DOG LOVER'S
INGLESE

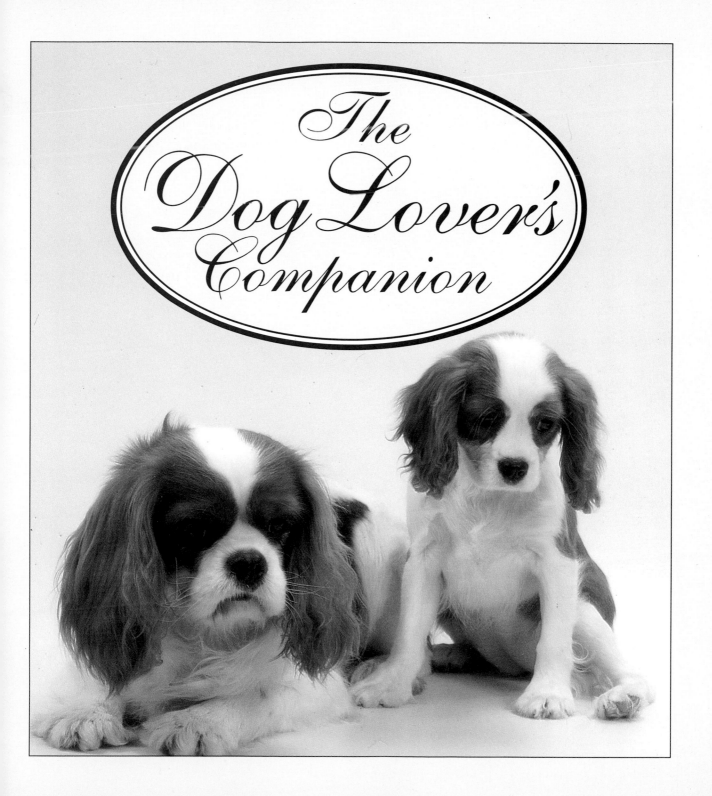

The Dog Lover's Companion

Dedication For Bunchie

Text and captions Richard Dawes

Astrology Louise Houghton

Editor Fleur Robertson

Design Claire Leighton

Photography Cogis Agency, Versailles, France

Illustrations Pam Martins; Terry Burton,courtesy of
Bernard Thornton Artists, London
(astrological cartoons)

Production Ruth Arthur; Sally Connolly,
Neil Randles, Jonathan Tickner

Director of Production Gerald Hughes

This edition published in 1994 by
Whitecap Books Ltd.
1086 West 3rd Street
North Vancouver, B.C.
Canada V7P 3J6
CLB 3396
© 1994 CLB Publishing Ltd, Godalming, Surrey, UK
Colour separations by Scantrans Pte Ltd, Singapore
Printed in Italy
ISBN 1-55110-115-7

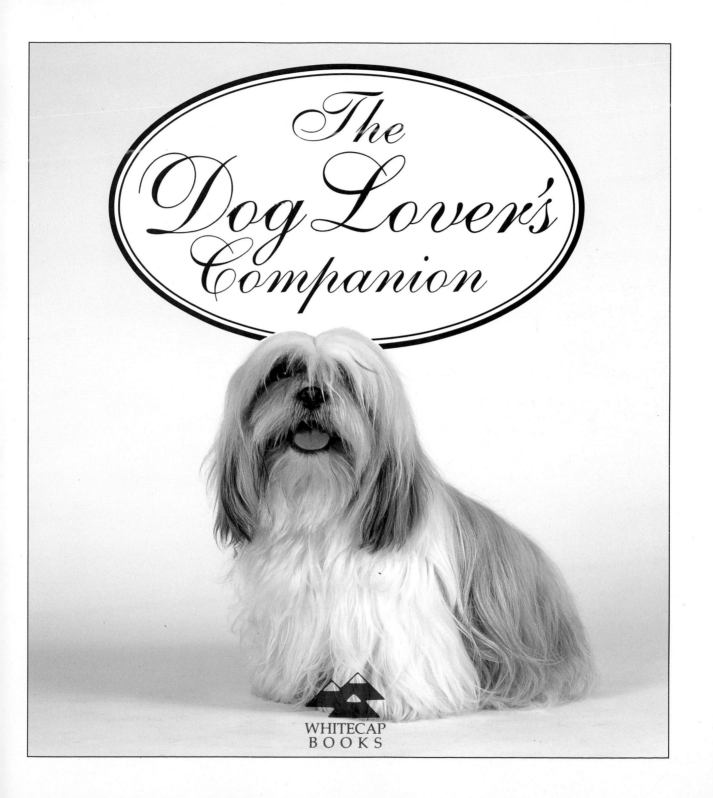

The Dog Lover's Companion

WHITECAP
BOOKS

~ *Introduction* ~

The Dog Lover's Companion is for dog lovers everywhere, whether
or not they own a dog. In the following pages there is a wealth of
dogs. Sensitively drawn and photographed, they come together to
form a wonderful collection, guaranteed to appeal to the great
range of their admirers, from the fans of toy dogs, such as the ever-
popular Yorkshire Terrier, to lovers of the mighty hounds, such as
the noble Great Dane. Particularly useful as a place to record the
special days of family friends – and pets! – this unique book is also a
colourful treasury of intriguing canine information, inviting to read
wherever the pages fall open.

Sympathetically designed throughout, *The Dog Lover's Companion*
is a must for all those happy people who are 'daft on dogs'.

An energetic little dog, the Basset Hound derives its name from the French for 'low': bas.

~ *January* ~

Ah! you should keep dogs – fine animals –
sagacious creatures – dog of my own once –
Pointer – surprising instinct – out shooting one day
– entering enclosure – whistled – dog stopped –
whistled again – Ponto – no go: stock still – called
him – Ponto, Ponto – wouldn't move – dog
transfixed – staring at a board – looked up, saw an
inscription – 'Gamekeeper has orders to shoot all
dogs found in this enclosure' – wouldn't pass it –
wonderful dog – valuable dog that – very.

Mr Jingles, in *The Pickwick Papers*,
Charles Dickens (1812-70)

The handsome English Setter is white flecked with black, liver or lemon, but sometimes has a tricolour coat.

~ January ~

~ 1 ~

DOG SNIPPETS

'Cynography' means the history of the dog.

~ 2 ~

~ 3 ~

~ 4 ~

~ 5 ~

~ 6 ~

~ 7 ~

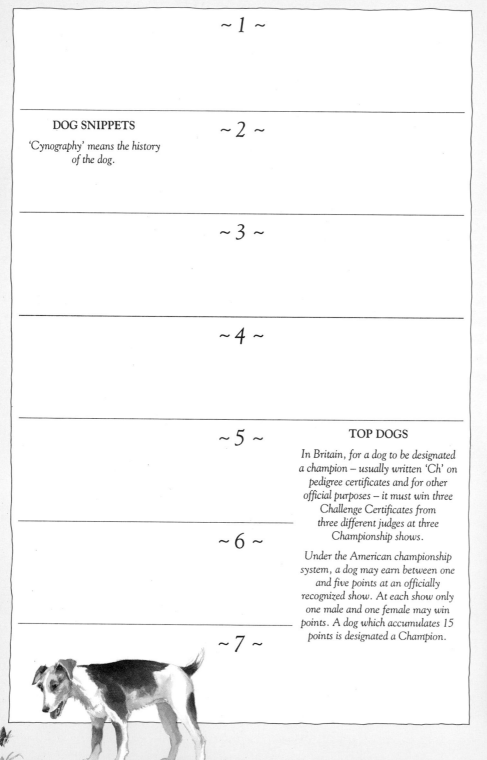

DOG FACTS

The duties of gundogs are divided between Pointers, Setters and Retrievers. The role of the first is to explore an area thoroughly with its keen sense of smell and 'point' to game with its nose.

Setters, like Pointers, rely heavily on their noses to locate game, which they then 'set' or 'put up', driving the birds into the air, where they can be shot at. Originally Spaniels were used for this purpose.

The Retriever's task is to bring back to the hunter game that has been killed or wounded. The dog's fleshy, soft mouth prevents the bird from being damaged by its teeth – a Retriever will instinctively carry a stick or newspaper with the same care.

TOP DOGS

In Britain, for a dog to be designated a champion – usually written 'Ch' on pedigree certificates and for other official purposes – it must win three Challenge Certificates from three different judges at three Championship shows.

Under the American championship system, a dog may earn between one and five points at an officially recognized show. At each show only one male and one female may win points. A dog which accumulates 15 points is designated a Champion.

The German Shorthaired Pointer is prized as an all-purpose gundog.

Excellent in the field, the German Shorthaired Pointer is also well suited to guarding the home.

~ 8 ~

~ 9 ~

~ 10 ~

~ 11 ~

~ 12 ~

~ 13 ~

~ 14 ~

DOGS IN HISTORY

Since long before recorded history, dogs have lent humankind protection, warmth, invaluable help in hunting and, perhaps most universally, companionship. In 1979, the remains of domestic dogs, dated by radiocarbon dating to around 12,000 BC, were found in the Middle East – evidence that the special bond of trust and fidelity between human and dog existed long before any other animal was tamed to meet human needs.

DOG BREEDS

Chow Chow

An ancient breed, whose origins date back more than 2,000 years, the Chow Chow is a member of the Polar or Spitz group of dogs. Like Huskies, Samoyeds, Alaskan Malamutes, Norwegian Elkhounds and other wolf-like dogs, it is a hardy creature with a thick coat and it is well suited to contending with strenuous work in extremely cold, even sub-Arctic, conditions. An unusual feature of the breed is its blue-black tongue.

A pair of Chow Chows taken from Canton, in southeast China, and used to start the breed in England, were described by the naturalist Gilbert White, in his Natural History of Selborne of 1789, as 'such as are fattened in that country for the purpose of being eaten'. Indeed bred at one time for the table by the Chinese, the Chow Chow is still considered a delicacy in parts of the Far East!

The impressively solid Chow Chow.

DOG DATA

The smallest breeds recognized by the Kennel Club of Great Britain are the Chihuahua and the Pekingese, both of which average 6-9in (15-23cm) in height. These, however, can dwarf the minuscule Chinese Imperial Ch'in, which is typically 3-6in (7.6-15cm) tall.

In the earliest Chinese chronicles the Chow Chow was referred to as the 'Tartar dog' or 'dog of the barbarians'.

DOG SAYINGS

The dog that's always on the go is better than the one that's always asleep
Irish proverb

~ 15 ~

~ 16 ~

~ 17 ~

~ 18 ~

~ 19 ~

~ 20 ~

~ 21 ~

DUTIFUL DOGS

Barry
Mention of the St Bernard evokes images of heroic mountain rescues amid swirling snowstorms. Barry, who lived with the monks of Switzerland's St Bernard monastery, epitomized that courage. Gifted with exceptional senses, he was able to alert the monks to imminent avalanches, and between 1800 and 1814 he rescued 40 snowbound travellers, including a child whose mother had just managed to strap him onto Barry's back before she died.

After his death Barry's successors as lead dog were given his name in honour of his bravery, and today Barry is preserved in Berne's National Museum.

DOG SNIPPETS

Dogs, or perhaps rather their owners, did not escape the off-the-wall wit of Groucho Marx (1895-1977), who said: 'Outside of a dog, a book is man's best friend. Inside a dog, it's too dark to read.'

Dedication personified: the St Bernard.

~ January ~

~ 22 ~

~ 23 ~

~ 24 ~

~ 25 ~

~ 26 ~

~ 27 ~

~ 28 ~

The Miniature Long-haired Dachshund should have a kind, intelligent expression.

~ 29 ~

~ 30 ~

DOG SAYINGS

He that strikes my dog
would strike me if he durst
Old Scottish proverb

~ 31 ~

DOGS IN HISTORY

In centuries past, drastic measures were taken to prevent dogs harming the royal hunt. For instance, William the Conqueror (1028-87) decreed that all dog owners should remove three toes from each foot of their animal to reduce its speed.

Centuries later French monarchs valued their hunting no less, for King François I (1494-1547) stipulated that 'a heavy block of wood' be attached to the heads of farmers' and peasants' dogs whenever the animals were away from their home. The king also decreed that any stray dog which hunted on royal land, even if it was wearing this impediment, would be hamstrung – that is, the large tendon at the back of the hock would be severed in each of its legs.

The fine head of a German Shepherd, alert even in repose.

Since cave-dwelling times, humankind has relied on hardy working dogs like the German Shepherd, or Alsatian.

~ *February* ~

The more I see of men the more I love dogs.

Attributed variously to Madame de Sévigné (1626-96)
and Frederick the Great of Prussia (1712-86)

The oldest of the Irish terrier breeds, the Soft-coated Wheaten Terrier, makes a fine companion and guard dog.

~ 1 ~

~ 2 ~

DOG DATA

It is estimated that there are around 140 million pet dogs in the world. Some 55 million of them are in the USA, while Britons keep almost 7.5 million dogs as pets.

~ 3 ~

~ 4 ~

~ 5 ~

~ 6 ~

~ 7 ~

DOG BREEDS

Chinese Crested Dog

Until recently one of the rarest breeds in the world, the Chinese Crested Dog is not the bizarre product of some modern experiment, but has a pedigree stretching back 3,000 years.

In 1966, Mrs Ruth Harris of Gloucestershire imported a number of Chinese Crested Dogs from an elderly lady in the USA who owned the only examples. Since then the breed has grown in popularity on both sides of the Atlantic, and is now shown and kept as a pet.

A striking feature of the dog is its hairless body – a feature it shares with the Mexican Hairless Dog, to which it is related. Equally strange is the contrasting abundance of hair on the head, a veritable mane, and on the feet and lower legs. A small breed, the Chinese Crested seldom weighs more than 12lb (5.5kg), while the bitch reaches 9-12in (23-30cm) in height and the dog 11-13in (28-33cm).

The eye-catching Chinese Crested Dog.

Extinct in its country of origin, the lively Chinese Crested Dog now has its enthusiasts in the West.

~ 8 ~

~ 9 ~

~ 10 ~

~ 11 ~

~ 12 ~

~ 13 ~

~ 14 ~

DOG SNIPPETS

The Cardigan Welsh Corgi is believed to be the oldest purebred British dog. One explanation of its origins is that Celts from the area around the Black Sea introduced the breed into Wales about 1200 BC, although this theory is disputed.

A Cardiganshire word for the dogs is 'Ci-llathed', or 'yard-long dog', a name which harks back to the original Cardigan Corgis. These were said to measure a Welsh yard – slightly longer than the English yard – from the tip of the nose to the tip of the tail.

A versatile working dog from the south and west of Ireland: the Kerry Blue Terrier.

DOG BREEDS

One account of the origins of the Kerry Blue Terrier, the national dog of Ireland, is that it is descended from white terrier-like dogs which somehow reached the Irish coast after the shipwreck of the Spanish armada in 1588. Another theory is that the strikingly be-whiskered dog is related to the much larger Irish Wolfhound.

The Kerry Blue is born black but in most cases turns blue-grey within 18 months. The breed was first shown in Britain in 1922, and officially recognized by the USA's Kennel Club two years later.

Traditionally the Welsh Cardigan Corgi was used to drive and herd dairy cows, wild steers and mountain ponies.

~ February ~

DOG TALES

Nana

In J. M. Barrie's (1860-1937) Peter Pan Nana is the faithful dog who keeps a constant watch over the Darling children. A prank of Mr Darling's – he gave Nana an unpleasant medicine that he had promised to take – backfired when the family failed to see the joke. To make matters worse, he fell into a sulk and chained Nana up before going out. Later, however, he himself came to understand what it means to be 'in the doghouse'. For, as a penance for the way he had treated Nana, he had to bed down in her kennel until the children returned.

~ 15 ~

~ 16 ~

~ 17 ~

~ 18 ~

~ 19 ~

~ 20 ~

~ 21 ~

TOP DOGS

The dogs internationally classified as Hounds have the keenest sense of smell. It is widely held that when performing their historic role of hunting they can distinguish between the scents of fear, exhaustion and anger given off by their prey.

Indisputably 'top dog' for its sense of smell is the Bloodhound. But also blessed with exceptionally good noses are the Basset Hound, the Foxhound, the Otterhound, the Norwegian Elkhound, Pointers and Setters, Labradors and Labrador Retrievers, the Alaskan Malamute and the Hungarian Vizsla. Other owners of refined, if not quite so acute, noses are dogs of the terrier group, the Cavalier King Charles Spaniel and indeed many mongrels.

The doleful-looking Basset Hound.

The Beagle is one of the oldest of all purebred British hounds.

~ 22 ~

~ 23 ~

TOP DOGS

Mick the Miller

The best known of all Greyhounds to race in Britain, Mick the Miller was born in Ireland in 1926 and lived to the grand old age – for a Greyhound – of 13. During a spectacular career he won two dog Derbys, came first or second in all but five of his 81 races in England and Ireland, and amassed £10,000 in prize money.

After his death Mick was stuffed and now can be seen in London's Natural History Museum. The postmortem revealed that the champion's heart weighed slightly more than the average for the breed. Yet whatever the effect of that extra ounce and a half (40g), it was the cheery nature of 'The Miller' just as much as his speed that delighted his many fans.

~ 24 ~

~ 25 ~

~ 26 ~

~ 27 ~

~ 28/29 ~

Taken to Britain by the Celts, the Greyhound is believed by some to be much earlier – almost as old as civilization itself.

DOGS IN HISTORY

Canute (995?-1035), King of England, Denmark and Norway, introduced a restriction on the ownership of dogs. He allowed only freemen, who formed a tiny minority of the population, to own Greyhounds, which were the favourite hunting dog of the time. This restriction lasted, in various forms, for some five centuries in England.

While other breeds of dog were in theory allowed to roam the royal forests, there were stringent legal restrictions on their size. To comply with the law, a dog had to be able to pass through a dog-measuring device of six inches in diameter. (One such measure, or stirrup, survives in the Hampshire village of Lyndhurst.) In practice this meant that the only dogs allowed to roam the royal hunting preserves were the smallest of breeds, which naturally posed little threat to the king's sport.

Like the Greyhound, the Whippet's lithe build and impressive speed make it ideal for track racing.

~ *March* ~

Now thou art dead, no eye shall ever see
For shape and service spaniel like to thee.
This shall my love do, give thy sad death one
Tear, that deserves of me a million.

'Upon my Spaniel, Tracie', Robert Herrick (1591-1674)

A Border Collie puppy finds its feet. The breed is valued as a sheepdog the world over.

~ March ~

~ 1 ~

~ 2 ~

~ 3 ~

DOG DATA

Fossil remains from the early Bronze Age, around 6500 years ago, have made it possible to identify five major groups of early dogs: Mastiffs, Greyhounds, Sheepdogs, Pointers and wolf-like dogs. Selective breeding and natural genetic mutation in these five groups produced the hundreds of breeds in existence today.

~ 4 ~

~ 5 ~

~ 6 ~

~ 7 ~

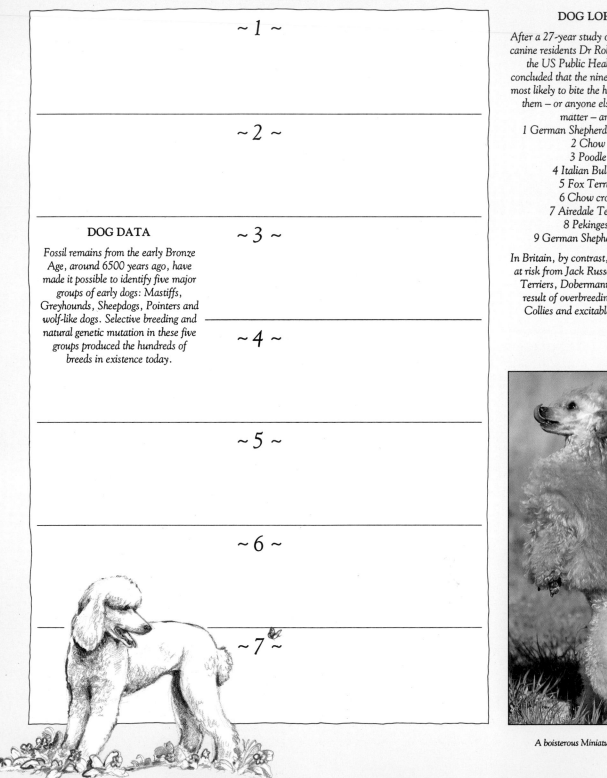

DOG LORE

After a 27-year study of New York's canine residents Dr Robert Oleson of the US Public Health Service concluded that the nine breeds of dog most likely to bite the hand that feeds them – or anyone else's for that matter – are:
1 German Shepherd (Alsatian)
2 Chow
3 Poodle
4 Italian Bulldog
5 Fox Terrier
6 Chow cross
7 Airedale Terrier
8 Pekingese
9 German Shepherd cross

In Britain, by contrast, you are most at risk from Jack Russells and other Terriers, Dobermanns and, as a result of overbreeding, pedigree Collies and excitable Spaniels.

A boisterous Miniature Poodle.

Both France and Germany claim Poodles — these two are a Standard mother and puppy — as a national breed.

~ 8 ~

~ 9 ~

~ 10 ~

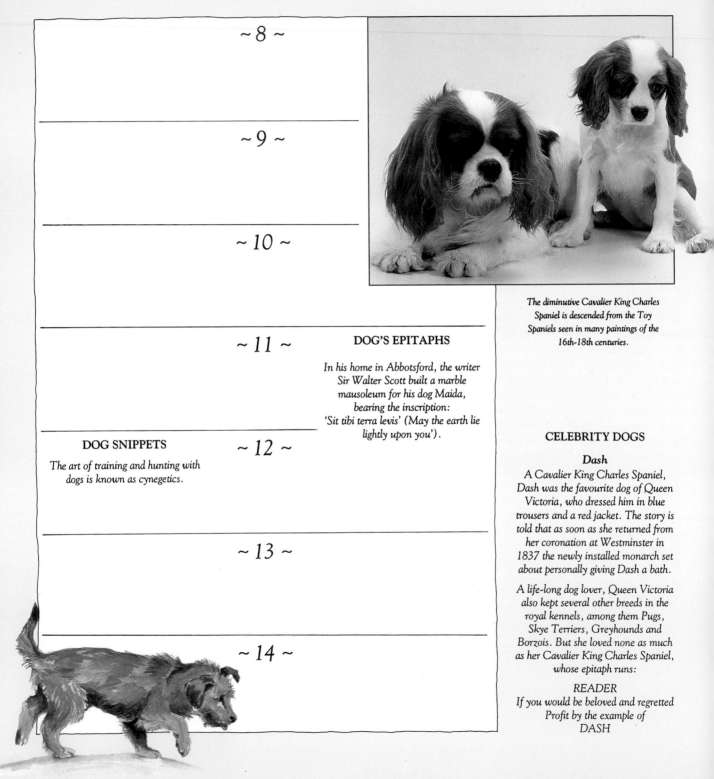

The diminutive Cavalier King Charles Spaniel is descended from the Toy Spaniels seen in many paintings of the 16th-18th centuries.

~ 11 ~

DOG'S EPITAPHS

In his home in Abbotsford, the writer Sir Walter Scott built a marble mausoleum for his dog Maida, bearing the inscription: 'Sit tibi terra levis' (May the earth lie lightly upon you').

DOG SNIPPETS

The art of training and hunting with dogs is known as cynegetics.

~ 12 ~

CELEBRITY DOGS

Dash

A Cavalier King Charles Spaniel, Dash was the favourite dog of Queen Victoria, who dressed him in blue trousers and a red jacket. The story is told that as soon as she returned from her coronation at Westminster in 1837 the newly installed monarch set about personally giving Dash a bath.

A life-long dog lover, Queen Victoria also kept several other breeds in the royal kennels, among them Pugs, Skye Terriers, Greyhounds and Borzois. But she loved none as much as her Cavalier King Charles Spaniel, whose epitaph runs:

READER
If you would be beloved and regretted
Profit by the example of
DASH

~ 13 ~

~ 14 ~

An appealing expression and a silky coat characterize the ever-popular Cavalier King Charles Spaniel.

DOG SAYINGS

Hold onto the bone and the dog will follow you
Dutch proverb

~ 15 ~

~ 16 ~

~ 17 ~

DOG SNIPPETS

The best kind of dog is the hot dog, because that's the only dog that feeds the hand that bites it
Anon

~ 18 ~

~ 19 ~

~ 20 ~

~ 21 ~

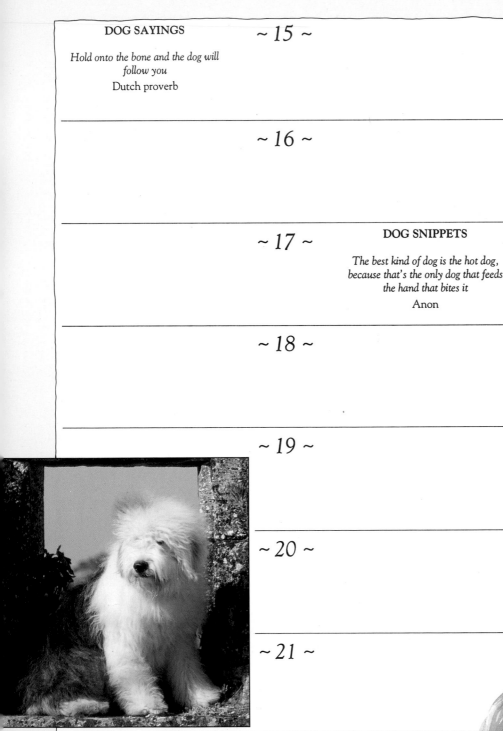

A lovable Old English Sheepdog puppy.

DEVOTED DOGS

Greyfriars Bobby

For fourteen years, Bobby watched over the grave of his master, the shepherd John Gray, in Edinburgh's Greyfriars Kirkyard. John Gray, or 'Auld Jock' as he was known, tended his flocks on the Pentland Hills south of the city, and when in Edinburgh, was a frequent diner, with Bobby, at the Greyfriars Dining Rooms.

After the shepherd's death, in 1858, Bobby stayed by his grave year after year, in all weathers, returning to it even after being ejected from the churchyard. He would only leave the grave at lunchtime each day, when he would go to the dining room and be fed by the owner, John Traill, who had been a good friend to Bobby's owner.

When Bobby died, in 1872, he was buried near the main entrance of Greyfriars Church, not far from the shepherd's grave. Today a stone, paid for by American admirers of Bobby, marks the grave of John Gray, and in nearby Candlemaker Row, a bronze statue of the faithful terrier crowns a drinking fountain. Bobby's memorial, erected by the Victorian philanthropist Baroness Burdett-Coutts, is a well-known landmark in Scotland's capital city.

The story of Greyfriars Bobby was made into a popular film of the same name by Walt Disney.

An intelligent herding dog, the Old English Sheepdog has a placid nature which makes it a fine friend for children.

~ 22 ~

DOG LORE

~ 23 ~

St Luke's Day, 18th October, is also known as Dog-whipping Day, because it is said that on that day a dog swallowed a consecrated wafer.

~ 24 ~

~ 25 ~

DOG SAYINGS

Better for a man to have even a dog welcome him home than growl at him
Polish proverb

~ 26 ~

~ 27 ~

~ 28 ~

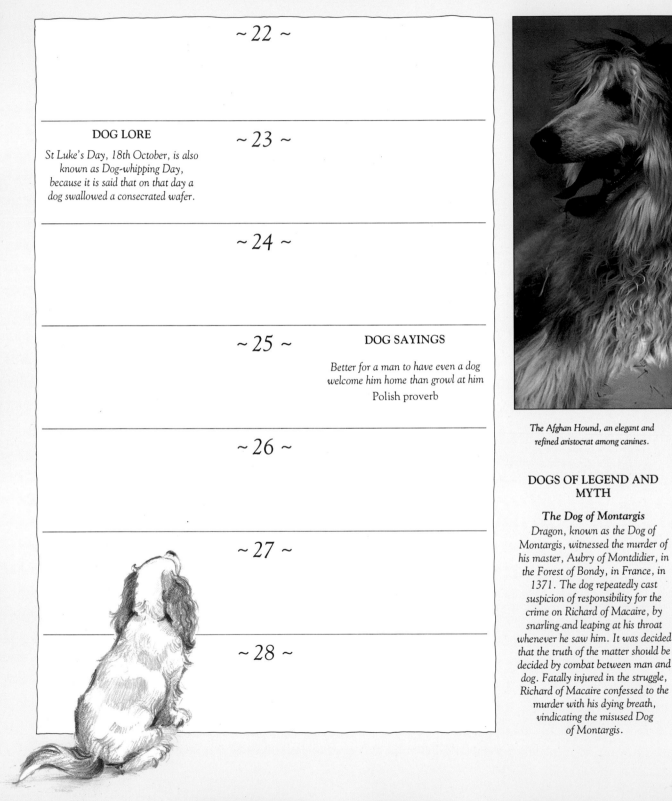

The Afghan Hound, an elegant and refined aristocrat among canines.

DOGS OF LEGEND AND MYTH

The Dog of Montargis

Dragon, known as the Dog of Montargis, witnessed the murder of his master, Aubry of Montdidier, in the Forest of Bondy, in France, in 1371. The dog repeatedly cast suspicion of responsibility for the crime on Richard of Macaire, by snarling and leaping at his throat whenever he saw him. It was decided that the truth of the matter should be decided by combat between man and dog. Fatally injured in the struggle, Richard of Macaire confessed to the murder with his dying breath, vindicating the misused Dog of Montargis.

In its mountainous country of origin the ancient Afghan Hound was historically a hunting and herding dog.

DOG SNIPPETS

I've got to see a man about a dog.
Dion Boucicault

In Boucicault's play, Flying Scud, a man trying to escape a lawyer who is accusing him of forgery claims he can't stay to continue the interview for this reason. The feebleness of the excuse caught the public's imagination and the phrase passed into the English language.

~ 29 ~

~ 30 ~

~ 31 ~

WRITERS' DOGS

John Steinbeck (1902-68) received some unusual but nevertheless persuasive literary criticism from his dog, Toby, when the Setter puppy chewed up half of the first draft of his novel Of Mice and Men.

However, the American novelist was lenient with the dog, partly because puppies have that effect on doting owners. But, as Steinbeck admitted, there was another compelling reason why he could not bring himself to punish the dog: he was himself undecided about the quality of the work.

When the draft received a poor reception from some of those who read it, Steinbeck was finally convinced that Toby had been right all along. Indeed, so impressed was he with the dog's critical acumen he proclaimed: 'I have promoted Toby-dog to be lieutenant-colonel in charge of literature.'

Keen, alert and ready to obey: two fine Red Setters.

Properly known as the Irish Setter, the Red Setter is blessed with a lustrous chestnut coat.

~ *April* ~

To his dog, every man is Napoleon; hence the
constant popularity of dogs.

Aldous Huxley (1894-1964)

The Wire Fox Terrier makes an intelligent family dog, whose hunting instincts need to be kept in check.

~ 1 ~

~ 2 ~

DOGS IN LEGEND AND MYTH

A familar Greek myth tells how the goddess Diana, angered at being surprised bathing naked by the hunter Actaeon, turned him into a stag, whereupon he was torn apart by his 50 dogs.

Less well known are the evocative names of Actaeon's pack of hounds, among whom were: Asbolos ('soot-coloured'), Cyllopotes ('zigzag runner'), Dromios ('seize 'em'), Harpiea ('tear 'em'), Lachne ('glossy-coated'), Lampos ('shining one'), Napa ('wolf-begotten'), Ocydroma ('swift runner'), Pamphagos ('ravenous'), Theridamas ('beast subduer') and Uranis ('heavenly one').

~ 3 ~

~ 4 ~

~ 5 ~

~ 6 ~

~ 7 ~

DOG BREEDS

Golden Retriever

This most good-natured of breeds has long been popular as the ideal family dog, so it may come as a surprise to learn that the breed has been with us for scarcely a century. Cruft's annual catalogue describes how, in 1868, Lord Tweedmouth mated a yellow Wavy-Coated Retriever called Nous to a Tweed Water-Spaniel named Belle. Over the next 22 years he methodically line-bred from this mating, using another Tweed Water-Spaniel, outcrosses of two black Retrievers, an Irish Setter and a sandy coloured Bloodhound.

Early this century one of the most influential kennels in England was founded on the products of Lord Tweedmouth's experiments and so was responsible for the worldwide spread of this golden variant of the Labrador Retriever.

Golden Retrievers vary in colour from the traditional chestnut brown to the more recent almost white.

Calm, kind and above all gentle, the Golden Retriever is the ideal dog for families with young children.

DOG DATA

The keenness of a dog's sense of smell varies according to breed. The 'rule of nose' is that the bigger the dog and the longer its muzzle, the keener its sense of smell. So, whereas an Alsatian (German Shepherd) has 200 million olfactory nerves, a Fox Terrier has about 150 million and a Dachshund about 125 million.

~ 8 ~

~ 9 ~

~ 10 ~

~ 11 ~

~ 12 ~

~ 13 ~

~ 14 ~

German Shepherd Dogs, beloved by millions.

A watchful German Shepherd.

DOG STARS

Benji

Fourteen years after being rescued from an animal sanctuary in California, Benji starred in the 1974 hit film named after him, in which he rescues two children who have been kidnapped. The lovable mongrel, who surely numbered at the least a Cocker Spaniel, a Schnauzer and a Poodle among his forebears, was too old for stardom when the sequel, For the Love of Benji, was being planned. The inspired solution was for one of his daughters to play his part, which she did so convincingly that she went on to enjoy television fame as Benji II.

German Shepherd puppies like this playful-looking youngster grow into the most loyal of canine companions.

~ 15 ~

~ 16 ~

~ 17 ~

Long-coat Chihuahuas.

DOG LORE

~ 18 ~

The Latin word for 'earth', terra, is the origin of the word 'terrier'. These indefatigable dogs well deserve the name, since they readily go to earth when hunting foxes, rabbits or badgers, and will happily enter the burrow to drive out the prey.

~ 19 ~

~ 20 ~

~ 21 ~

DOGS ON SHOW

Cruft's, Britain's best-known dog show, was the idea of Charles Cruft, a resourceful salesman employed in late-Victorian times by the dog-food manufacturer James Spratt.

In the 1870s Cruft came back from the USA with an idea that led to production of the highly successful Spratt's Dog Cakes. Around the same time, while on business in France, he became involved in promoting a dog show, and over the following years became ever more aware of the growing interest among Britons in breeding pedigree dogs. Eventually, in 1891, this trend encouraged him to book London's imposing Royal Agricultural Hall for a private dog show.

Such was the show's success that it became an annual fixture, and after Cruft's death in 1938 his widow held one more show. Cruft's Dog Show then ceased until 1948, when the Kennel Club of Great Britain took over its running, organizing shows every year since then, with a few exceptions.

Small enough to be a lap-dog, the Chihuahua is nevertheless fierce enough to afford its owner protection.

~ April ~

~ 22 ~

~ 23 ~

~ 24 ~

~ 25 ~

~ 26 ~

~ 27 ~

~ 28 ~

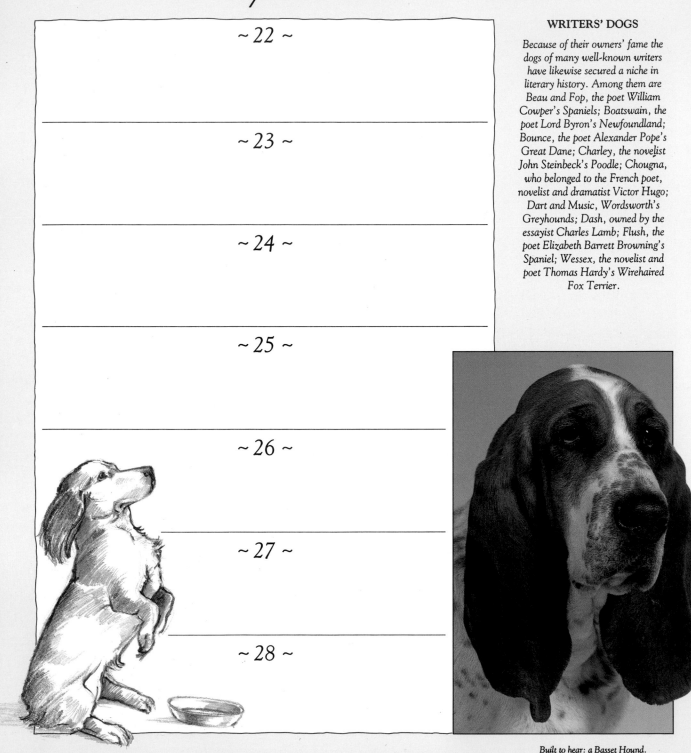

WRITERS' DOGS

Because of their owners' fame the dogs of many well-known writers have likewise secured a niche in literary history. Among them are Beau and Fop, the poet William Cowper's Spaniels; Boatswain, the poet Lord Byron's Newfoundland; Bounce, the poet Alexander Pope's Great Dane; Charley, the novelist John Steinbeck's Poodle; Chougna, who belonged to the French poet, novelist and dramatist Victor Hugo; Dart and Music, Wordsworth's Greyhounds; Dash, owned by the essayist Charles Lamb; Flush, the poet Elizabeth Barrett Browning's Spaniel; Wessex, the novelist and poet Thomas Hardy's Wirehaired Fox Terrier.

Built to hear: a Basset Hound.

The forefathers of Basset Hound, a cross between the French Basset and the Bloodhound, are evident in its head.

~ *April* ~

~ 29 ~

DOG SAYINGS

~ 30 ~

*Three things are not to be trusted;
a cow's horn, a dog's tooth
and a horse's hoof*
Irish saying

DOG SNIPPETS

The term 'hot dog' was coined by the American sports cartoonist T. A. 'Tad' Dorgan, who satirized the new craze for eating frankfurters in a long bread roll, first seen in 1906, in New York, by depicting a Dachshund served up in this manner.

For a while many New Yorkers feared that the snack actually contained dog meat, and a ban on the term was imposed by the local Chamber of Commerce. But you can't keep a good name down, and it bounced back into popular use. Nowadays it seems unthinkable that at one time you couldn't ask for a 'hot dog' without breaking the law.

A bright-eyed little 'Westie'.

First bred from white puppies in a Cairn Terrier litter, the West Highland White Terrier is now a firm favourite.

~ *May* ~

Brothers and Sisters, I bid you beware
Of giving your heart to a dog to tear.

'The Power of a Dog', Rudyard Kipling (1865-1936)

A Pomeranian double act: a 'straight man' and a comedian.

~ May ~

~ 1 ~

~ 2 ~

DOGS IN LEGEND AND MYTH

According to an Irish legend, the Devil's dog lies in wait for sinners to die, and then pursues their souls to punish their wickedness.

~ 3 ~

~ 4 ~

~ 5 ~

~ 6 ~

~ 7 ~

TOP DOGS

Lena, an American Foxhound, is said to have borne a litter of 23 puppies – the record for any breed of dog – in 1944. However, controversy has always surrounded the claim, for the puppies were not registered, and may have come from more than one litter.

A St Bernard also produced 23, but 11 died while an application was being made to register the birth.

Among records for other breeds is that set by the Irish Setter Emma, who produced litters of 18, 16 and 15 puppies in 1981, 1982 and 1983. The largest Great Dane litter registered by the American Kennel Club is 19, although a litter of 21 has also been claimed. The AKC's record for the Dobermann is 17. In 1917 a Bloodhound produced 17 puppies, all of which survived.

Several breeds have given birth to litters of 16, including the English Setter, English Springer Spaniel, Chesapeake Bay Retriever, Alsatian (German Shepherd) and Golden Retriever. Litters of 15 puppies have been born to a number of breeds, including the Airedale, Boxer, Bouvier de Flandres, Brittany Spaniel, Dalmatian, Irish Water-Spaniel, Labrador Retriever and Poodle.

A Dobermann with perfect poise.

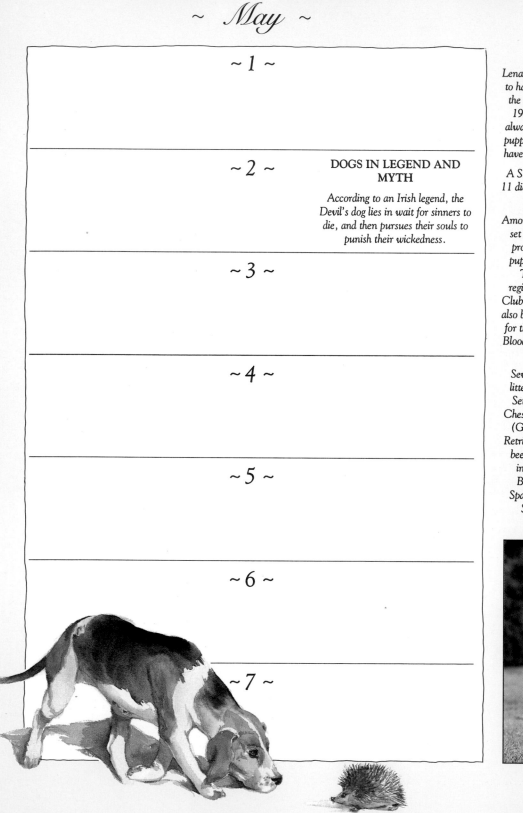

Among the finest of guard dogs, the Dobermann proves a responsive and affectionate companion if trained well.

~ 8 ~

~ 9 ~

~ 10 ~

DOG SAYINGS

Strike a dog with a bone and
he'll not growl
    Irish proverb

~ 11 ~

~ 12 ~

~ 13 ~

~ 14 ~

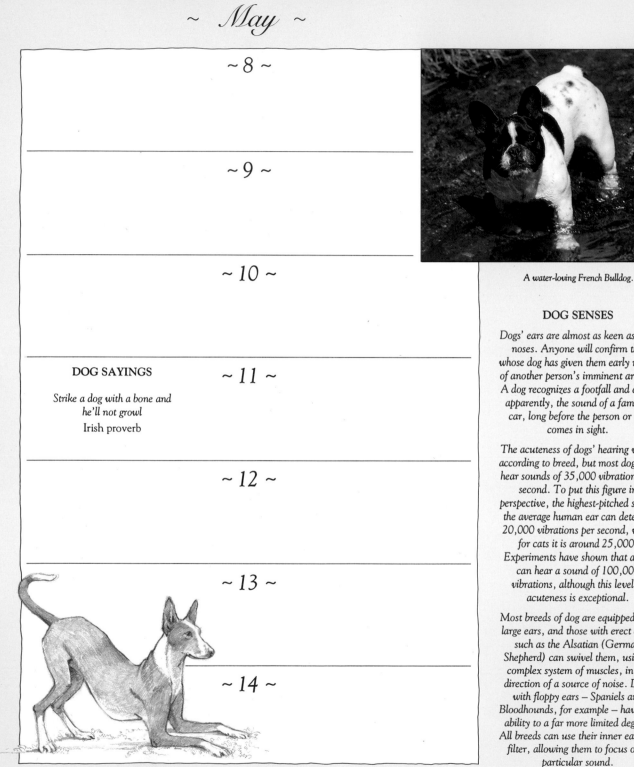

A water-loving French Bulldog.

DOG SENSES

Dogs' ears are almost as keen as their noses. Anyone will confirm this whose dog has given them early notice of another person's imminent arrival. A dog recognizes a footfall and even, apparently, the sound of a familiar car, long before the person or car comes in sight.

The acuteness of dogs' hearing varies according to breed, but most dogs can hear sounds of 35,000 vibrations per second. To put this figure in perspective, the highest-pitched sound the average human ear can detect is 20,000 vibrations per second, while for cats it is around 25,000. Experiments have shown that a dog can hear a sound of 100,000 vibrations, although this level of acuteness is exceptional.

Most breeds of dog are equipped with large ears, and those with erect ears, such as the Alsatian (German Shepherd) can swivel them, using a complex system of muscles, in the direction of a source of noise. Dogs with floppy ears – Spaniels and Bloodhounds, for example – have this ability to a far more limited degree. All breeds can use their inner ear as a filter, allowing them to focus on a particular sound.

Held by the British to be descended from their Bulldog, in France the French Bulldog is seen as a national breed.

~ *May* ~

TOP DOGS

Travelling as a canine companion in the Soviet manned satellite Sputnik II in 1957, a Samoyed bitch known variously as Kudryavka (Curly), Limonchik (Little Lemon) and Laika (Husky) penetrated 1050 miles (1690 km) into space – the greatest altitude reached by a mammal other than a human.

~ 15 ~

~ 16 ~

~ 17 ~

~ 18 ~

~ 19 ~

~ 20 ~

~ 21 ~

DEVOTED DOGS

A Welsh folk tale dating from the 13th century tells how Prince Llewelyn returned to his castle to find his baby son missing and the jaws of his dog Gelert, whom he had entrusted with guarding the boy, dripping with blood.

After the distraught prince had put the hound to death with his sword, he had a further cruel shock, for he found his son alive near the body of a large wolf which the faithful Gelert had clearly killed.

A nearby village is named Beddgelert, or Gelert's Grave, and the reputed grave of Prince Llewelyn's courageous wolfhound, situated in a field near the picturesque Mount Snowdon, can be visited.

A Japanese Spitz with her puppies.

The robust little Japanese Spitz belongs to the group of dogs which include Huskies and other cold-climate breeds.

~ May ~

~ 22 ~

~ 23 ~

~ 24 ~

~ 25 ~

~ 26 ~

~ 27 ~

~ 28 ~

DOG DATA

Domesticated dogs belong to the same animal grouping, or genus, as wolves, foxes, jackals and coyotes. Dogs are classified as 'Canis familiaris', meaning 'domestic dog'.

The genus Canis started to evolve some ten million years ago, but within this grouping the wolf, Canis lupus, evolved relatively recently, only half a million years ago. The wolf is believed by some to be the ancestor of the domestic dog, but this has yet to be proven conclusively.

A keen-nosed American Cocker Spaniel.

Her serious face belies the breed's nickname 'the merry Cocker', but maybe this bitch is just feeling protective.

~ May ~

~ 29 ~

~ 30 ~

~ 31 ~

DOG SNIPPETS

Not the least hard thing to bear when they go away from us, these quiet friends, is that they carry away with them so many years of our own lives.
John Galsworthy

A handsome Weimaraner at rest.

The Weimaraner's colour is its most striking feature: a lustrous pale grey, often with a hint of pink.

~ *June* ~

Here lies one, who never drew
Blood himself, yet many slew ...
Stout he was, and large of limb,
Scores fled at sight of him;
And to all this fame he rose
Only following his nose.

'An *Epitaph*', William Cowper (1731-1800)

Cross-breeding of the King Charles Spaniel produced the larger and longer-legged Cavalier King Charles.

~ *June* ~

~ 1 ~

~ 2 ~

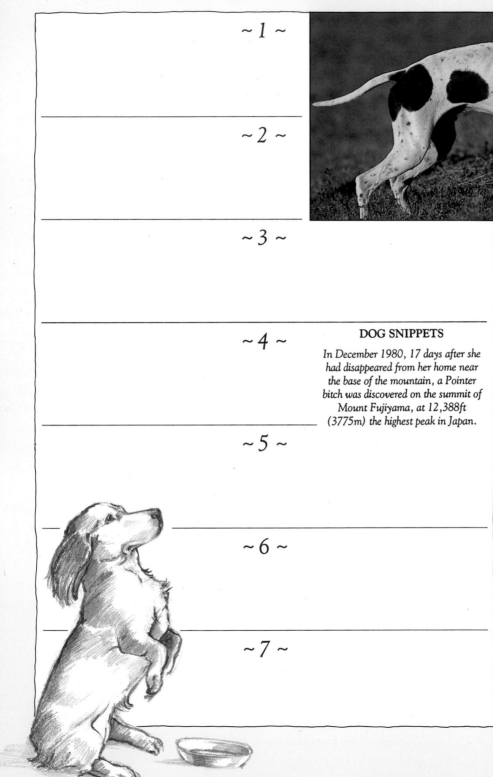

The lean lines of a healthy Pointer.

~ 3 ~

~ 4 ~

DOG SNIPPETS

In December 1980, 17 days after she had disappeared from her home near the base of the mountain, a Pointer bitch was discovered on the summit of Mount Fujiyama, at 12,388ft (3775m) the highest peak in Japan.

~ 5 ~

~ 6 ~

~ 7 ~

DOG STARS

Rin Tin Tin

Destined to become the most hallowed of all canine movie stars, Rin Tin Tin was rescued as a pup by American soldiers from a German dug-out in France during World War One. The Alsatian (German Shepherd) was taken to California, where he began a career in the public eye by appearing in dog shows. So successful was his acting debut, in the 1923 film Where the North Begins, that before his death in 1932 he made over 40 more, proving a godsend to Warner Brothers.

Rin Tin Tin's feats – which included scaling walls fitted with hidden footholds, crashing through 'glass' made of clear sugar and running through flames while coated with fireproof substances – brought him ten thousand letters a week from adoring fans and earnings of over a million dollars.

The legend lived on: in the 1930s through films starring Rin Tin Tin Junior, through the 1947 film The Return of Rin Tin Tin, featuring another of his descendants, and from 1954 through the highly popular television series The Adventures of Rin Tin Tin .

Originating in mainland Europe, the Pointer was improved last century by the addition of English Pointer blood.

~ June ~

CELEBRITY DOGS

Diamond

When Sir Isaac Newton's dog knocked over a candle and set fire to the records of years of experiments, the great scientist was a model of masterly restraint, saying : 'Oh, Diamond, Diamond, thou little knowest the mischief thou hast done', before setting to work to make good the loss.

~ 8 ~

~ 9 ~

~ 10 ~

DOG SAYINGS

An old dog will learn no new tricks
Thomas D'Urfey

~ 11 ~

~ 12 ~

~ 13 ~

~ 14 ~

DOG DATA

A dog's eyesight is not as important to it as its sense of smell and hearing, since it mainly hunts, and orientates itself, with its nose and ears. In fact, dogs' eyes are typically weaker in daylight than a human's, although at night they are far keener, for in the wild dogs have always hunted by night, complementing their keen nose and ears with their eyes.

Scientists disagree on whether dogs can see in colour, but the predominant verdict is that they are almost colour-blind, seeing only in black, white and shades of grey. It is also widely accepted that a dog sees things indistinctly, identifying a person or object by the basic shape, and confirming its findings with its nose and ears.

What's up? wonders this Airedale pup.

Bred expressly for the long-dead sport of otter hunting, as a pet the Airedale remains a sturdy and tenacious dog.

~ 15 ~

~ 16 ~

~ 17 ~

~ 18 ~

~ 19 ~

~ 20 ~

~ 21 ~

DOG TALES

Eleanor Ritchey of Florida left eight million pounds to her dogs when she died. Under the terms of the will the money was eventually to go to Auburn University's School of Veterinary Science, but only when every one of the dogs had passed away. The problem for the ultimate beneficiaries was that Eleanor Ritchey's love of dogs had been so great that there were 150 of them at the time of her death in 1968. By the end of 1983, only one dog, Musketeer, was still hanging on to life. However, so weak was he that he fell over every time he sneezed, so it was not long before the handsome legacy at last reached its intended destination, where it could help Musketeer's fellow animals.

The fine head of a Borzoi.

DOGS IN HISTORY

It is believed that the Greyhound first arrived in Europe in medieval times, on Phoenician trading ships from the Middle East. Its speed soon made it a favourite with royal and noble hunters, and the esteem in which the breed was held is reflected in its frequent appearance in heraldry. Among the monarchs who used the image of the Greyhound in their coat of arms were Henry VIII of England and Charles V of France.

The Greyhound belongs to the group of dogs known by the ancient term 'gazehounds', because they were trained to hunt by sight. Although it is among the oldest of such hunting breeds, the Saluki, from the Middle East, may be older. Other gazehounds are the Whippet, Collie, Borzoi and Afghan Hound.

The Borzoi, widely regarded as the most aristocratic of hounds, was originally used in Russia to hunt wolves.

~ 22 ~

~ 23 ~

~ 24 ~

DOG SNIPPETS

The term 'cynorexia', meaning an appetite like that of a dog, is used to describe insatiable hunger.

~ 25 ~

~ 26 ~

~ 27 ~

~ 28 ~

DOG SNIPPETS

The national breed of the Netherlands, the Keeshond, is named after Jan Kees, the Dutch equivalent of Britain's John Smith or the USA's John Doe. The early Dutch settlers in America were known as 'Jan Kees', from which the term 'Yankees' is derived.

The Keeshond, the Dutch national breed.

As the traditional protector of canal boats, the powerful Keeshond was nicknamed the 'Dutch barge dog'.

~ 29 ~

When the dog-loving English monarch
Charles II (1630-85), after whom
the Cavalier King Charles Spaniel is
named, lost his dog, in desperation he
placed the following plaintive plea in a
newspaper of the day, the
Mercurius Publicus:
'We must call upon you again for a
black dog, between a greyhound and a
spaniel, no white about him, only a
streak on his breast, and his tail a little
bobbed. It is his Majesty's own dog,
and doubtless was stolen, for the dog
was not born or bred in England, and
would never forsake his master.
Whosoever finds him may acquaint
any at Whitehall, for the dog was
better known at court than those who
stole him: Will they never leave off
robbing his Majesty? Must he not
keep a dog?

DOG SAYINGS

~ 30 ~

*It's like looking for a hound
without knowing its colour*
Irish saying

But for Edward VII's disapproval, the King Charles Spaniel might now be called the Toy Spaniel.

A Cavalier King Charles Spaniel poses as if for Van Dyck, who painted King Charles I with his beloved dogs.

~ *July* ~

I am called a dog because I fawn on those
who give me anything,
I yelp at those who refuse,
and I set my teeth in rascals.

Diogenes (c. 412-323 BC)

A Miniature Poodle puppy sizes up an unexplored world of sights, sounds and smells.

~ July ~

~ 1 ~

~ 2 ~

~ 3 ~

~ 4 ~

~ 5 ~

~ 6 ~

~ 7 ~

FICTIONAL DOGS

Perdita

A lovable character in Dodie Smith's 1956 story The Hundred and One Dalmatians, which was made into a film by Walt Disney, is Perdita, a Dalmatian with liver-coloured spots.

Perdita helped to nurse the 15 puppies produced by Mrs Dearly's Dalmatian Missis, but when her milk ran out, the rescued stray – whose name is Latin for 'lost' – feared she would be thrown out.

Far from ejecting Perdita, however, Mrs Dearly was so impressed with her washing of the pups that she assured her that she could scarcely manage without her. To celebrate her joy at being allowed to stay, Perdita washed every one of the puppies once again.

Dalmatians' spots are black or liver.

With hunting dogs as its forebears, the modern Dalmatian remains very active and requires plenty of exercise.

~ *July* ~

~ 8 ~

~ 9 ~

~ 10 ~

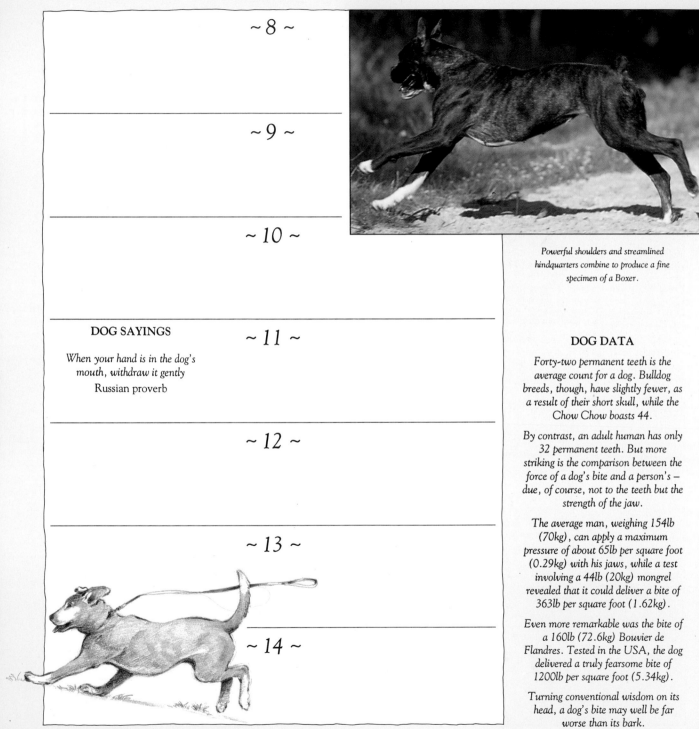

Powerful shoulders and streamlined hindquarters combine to produce a fine specimen of a Boxer.

DOG SAYINGS

When your hand is in the dog's mouth, withdraw it gently
Russian proverb

~ 11 ~

~ 12 ~

~ 13 ~

~ 14 ~

DOG DATA

Forty-two permanent teeth is the average count for a dog. Bulldog breeds, though, have slightly fewer, as a result of their short skull, while the Chow Chow boasts 44.

By contrast, an adult human has only 32 permanent teeth. But more striking is the comparison between the force of a dog's bite and a person's – due, of course, not to the teeth but the strength of the jaw.

The average man, weighing 154lb (70kg), can apply a maximum pressure of about 65lb per square foot (0.29kg) with his jaws, while a test involving a 44lb (20kg) mongrel revealed that it could deliver a bite of 363lb per square foot (1.62kg).

Even more remarkable was the bite of a 160lb (72.6kg) Bouvier de Flandres. Tested in the USA, the dog delivered a truly fearsome bite of 1200lb per square foot (5.34kg).

Turning conventional wisdom on its head, a dog's bite may well be far worse than its bark.

Their personalities already emerging, a litter of Boxer puppies adopt a variety of stances.

~ 15 ~

DOG SNIPPETS

The plucky little Dandie Dinmont Terrier, which originated in the border country between England and Scotland, owes its name to a dog-loving farmer in Sir Walter Scott's (1771-1832) novel Guy Mannering.

~ 16 ~

~ 17 ~

~ 18 ~

~ 19 ~

~ 20 ~

~ 21 ~

DEVOTED DOGS

The first 'Hearing Dog' centre in the world was set up in San Francisco in 1977, after a pilot scheme initiated the previous year by the American Humane Association. Since then a growing number of deaf people have achieved greater mobility and independence by having a Hearing Dog to act as ears for them, identifying everyday sounds and warning of danger from, for example, traffic. A dog can even be trained to alert a deaf mother to the fact that her baby is crying.

In 1982 the Hearing Dog scheme was introduced into Britain, where the dogs wear an orange collar and lead, are entitled to free veterinary care and travel free of charge on specified road, rail and internal airline services.

Dogs of all kinds are trained to help the deaf, but one thing they have in common is that they were all unwanted animals, most of them in animal sanctuaries, before being selected to become Hearing Dogs.

A rigorous assessment of a candidate's temperament and intelligence, accompanied by medical examinations, precedes acceptance on the training course, which lasts four months. Part of the course involves the replacement of verbal commands by hand signals, to help the deaf person who has speech difficulties. For a week or so after the dog has been assigned to its new home, a counsellor visits to check that the arrangement is working well for both owner and dog.

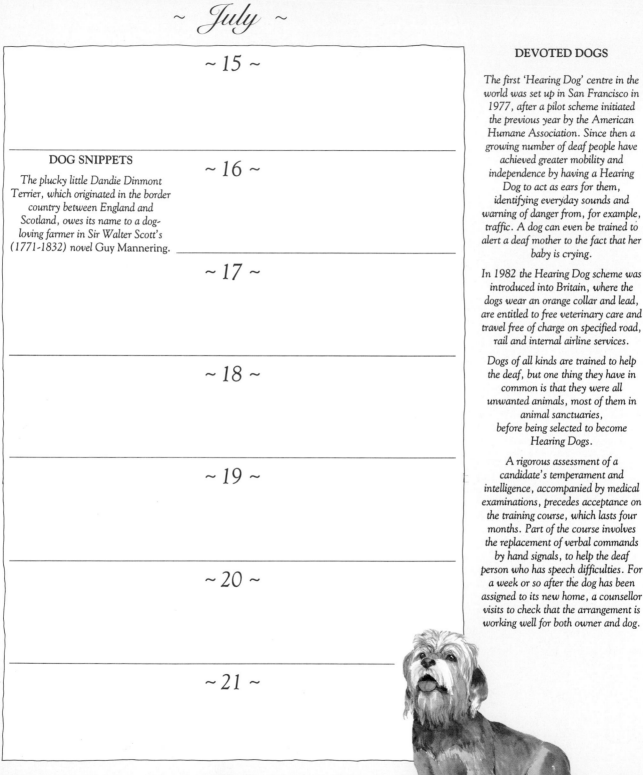

Along with his courage and devotion, the Dandie Dinmont Terrier's deep bark makes him an ideal house dog.

~ *July* ~

DOG SNIPPETS

Many have lamented the fact that a dog's lifespan is so much shorter than that of its owner. But few have given this sentiment such heartfelt and succinct expression as the writer Sir Walter Scott, who wrote: 'The misery of keeping a dog is his dying so soon. But, to be sure, if he lived for 50 years and then died, what would become of me?'

~ 22 ~

~ 23 ~

~ 24 ~

~ 25 ~

~ 26 ~

~ 27 ~

~ 28 ~

CELEBRITY DOGS

Flush

Elizabeth Barrett Browning, the wife of another Victorian poet, Robert Browning, received the gift of a Spaniel from a friend. Her unabashed devotion to the dog, whom she named Flush, was to become the subject of many letters and poems.

In one such poem, 'Flush or Faunus', she recalls how the dog disturbed her reverie, deceiving her into thinking for a moment that a faun (a rural deity in Roman England) had brushed her cheek. When she realized that it was instead Flush's whiskery face, she rejoiced to see the beloved dog rather than an imaginary figure, and thanked the god Pan, 'Who, by low creatures, leads to heights of love.'

A snow-loving Glen of Imaal Terrier.

A fine working dog and good with children: the Glen of Imaal Terrier, which originated in Co. Wicklow, Ireland.

~ *July* ~

~ 29 ~

DOG SNIPPETS

*He cannot be a gentleman
which loveth not a dog*
John Northbrooke

~ 30 ~

~ 31 ~

DOG BREEDS

The Chesapeake Bay Retriever came into being as the result of a shipwreck off Maryland in 1807. Rescued from the ship were two puppies, probably Newfoundlands, called Canton and Sailor. One was red and the other black, and they were later mated with local dogs, including both Flat-Coated and Curly-Coated Retrievers, and possibly other breeds.

The product was the Chesapeake Bay Retriever. A brave, robust dog, it is an excellent swimmer, and is well equipped for the purpose with its gundog's webbed feet and an oily, coarse-haired coat that repels water wonderfully.

A trio of working Chesapeake Bay Retrievers in the field, every ounce of attention focused on the task in hand.

Fans of the Chesapeake Bay Retriever are resisting its becoming just another pet, preferring to see the breed work.

~ *August* ~

The great pleasure of a dog is that you may make a
fool of yourself with him and not only will he not
scold you, but he will make a fool of himself too.

Samuel Butler (1835-1902)

Its double coat recalls the Bearded Collie's former role as a cattle dog in Scotland.

~ August ~

~ 1 ~

~ 2 ~

DOG SNIPPETS

~ 3 ~

'Cynolyssa' is a synonym for hydrophobia, the fear of water associated with rabies. Incidentally, it is not true that a dog suffering from rabies is afraid of water. The fact is that a symptom of the disease is the inability to eat and drink, which is why a rabid dog shuns water.

~ 4 ~

~ 5 ~

~ 6 ~

~ 7 ~

CELEBRITY DOGS

Wessex

The subject of three poems written by Thomas Hardy in the 1920s, when the novelist was in his eighties, was his second wife's Wirehaired Fox Terrier. Allowed on the dining table during meals, Wessex quite understandably challenged guests' right to their own food. If indulgence on his owners' part explains the dog's table manners, it probably accounts too for his habit of intimidating servants and attacking postmen and visitors alike. Certainly the writer is convinced that the dog himself does not know why he does it, for he puts the following words in his mouth:

' I live here: Wessex is my name;
I am a dog known rather well:
I guard the house; but how that came
To be my whim I cannot tell.'

Wessex died in 1926 at the age of 13.

Wirehaired Fox Terriers enjoy a romp.

Fearless and determined, the Wirehaired Fox Terrier can be gentle too, with people he knows.

~ 8 ~

~ 9 ~

~ 10 ~

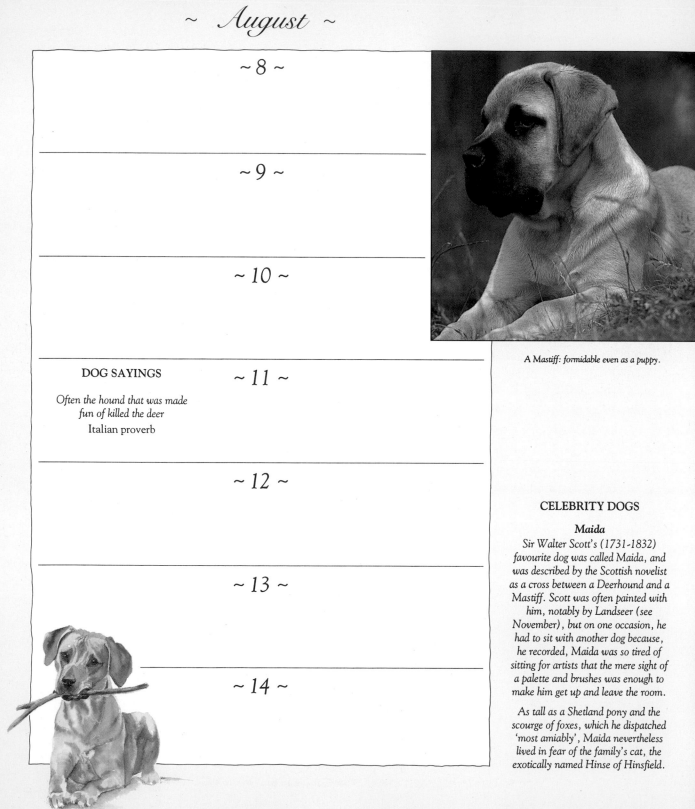

A Mastiff: formidable even as a puppy.

DOG SAYINGS

*Often the hound that was made
fun of killed the deer*
Italian proverb

~ 11 ~

~ 12 ~

~ 13 ~

~ 14 ~

CELEBRITY DOGS

Maida

Sir Walter Scott's (1731-1832)
favourite dog was called Maida, and
was described by the Scottish novelist
as a cross between a Deerhound and a
Mastiff. Scott was often painted with
him, notably by Landseer (see
November), but on one occasion, he
had to sit with another dog because,
he recorded, Maida was so tired of
sitting for artists that the mere sight of
a palette and brushes was enough to
make him get up and leave the room.

As tall as a Shetland pony and the
scourge of foxes, which he dispatched
'most amiably', Maida nevertheless
lived in fear of the family's cat, the
exotically named Hinse of Hinsfield.

Over the centuries the ancient Mastiff has been tranformed from a fighting dog into a dependable companion.

~ *August* ~

~ 15 ~

~ 16 ~

DOGS IN HISTORY

So besotted with dogs was King Henry III of France (1551-89) that even on solemn occasions he would sometimes wear suspended from his neck a basket trimmed with ribbons and carrying several little Papillons. This toy breed, whose name means 'butterfly', probably on account of its wing-shaped ears, averages 8-11in (20-28cm) in height.

~ 17 ~

~ 18 ~

~ 19 ~

~ 20 ~

~ 21 ~

DEVOTED DOGS

Hachiko

Japan has its counterpart to Greyfriars Bobby (see March) in Hachiko. The Akita accompanied his master to the railway station every morning, and went back in the evening to meet him on his return from Tokyo University, where he was a professor.

One afternoon in 1925 the academic died of a heart attack, but at 5pm that day the dog was, as usual, at Shibuya station, waiting patiently for him. Clinging to the hope that his owner would return, Hachiko went to the station every evening at the customary time, until his death in 1935.

The Japanese took the loyal dog to their hearts, and honoured his memory by erecting a statue of him at the place where he had always waited for the professor.

A Briard with its typically coarse coat.

Probably the most ancient of the French Sheepdogs, the Briard is an alert and biddable breed.

~ 22 ~

~ 23 ~

~ 24 ~

~ 25 ~

~ 26 ~

~ 27 ~

~ 28 ~

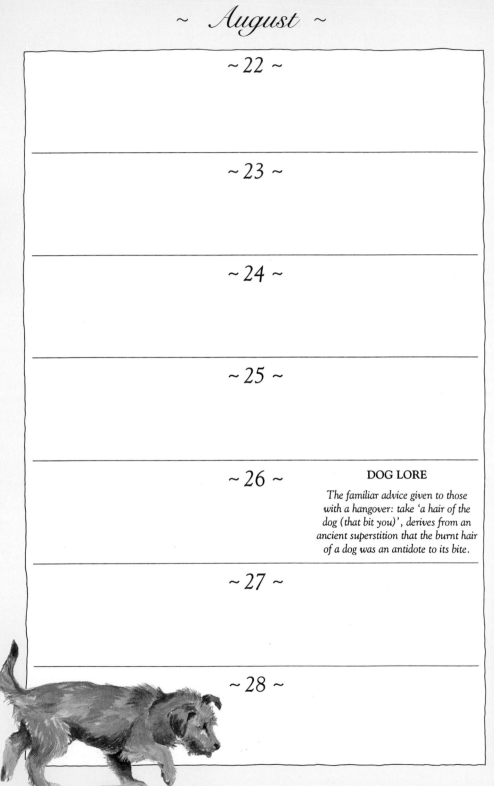

DOG SNIPPETS

The Bulldog has long been associated, if somewhat romantically, with British determination, but there is a less savoury aspect to its history. It was an English nobleman, Earl Warren of Stamford, who conceived the idea of the sport of bull-baiting when, in 1209, he watched two Bulldogs contend with a bull. The practice flourished in Britain until it was outlawed in 1838.

DOG LORE

The familiar advice given to those with a hangover: take 'a hair of the dog (that bit you)', derives from an ancient superstition that the burnt hair of a dog was an antidote to its bite.

A Bulldog enjoys a joke. . .

But this one doesn't!

~ 29 ~

~ 30 ~

DOG DATA

The tallest breeds of dog are the Great Dane and the Irish Wolfhound, which can grow to 41in (104cm) and 39in (100cm) respectively.

~ 31 ~

DOGS IN HISTORY

A cart drawn by dogs may seem like the obvious definition of the term 'dog cart', and such conveyances did in fact exist. However, in Victorian and Edwardian times it usually meant a light, one-horse trap used to carry gundogs.

Perhaps a rest is a better idea!

DOG DATA

Six main groups of dogs are recognized internationally for purposes of showing. The Kennel Club of Great Britain defines these groups as: Hounds, Gundogs, Terriers, Utility Dogs, Working Dogs and Toy Dogs.

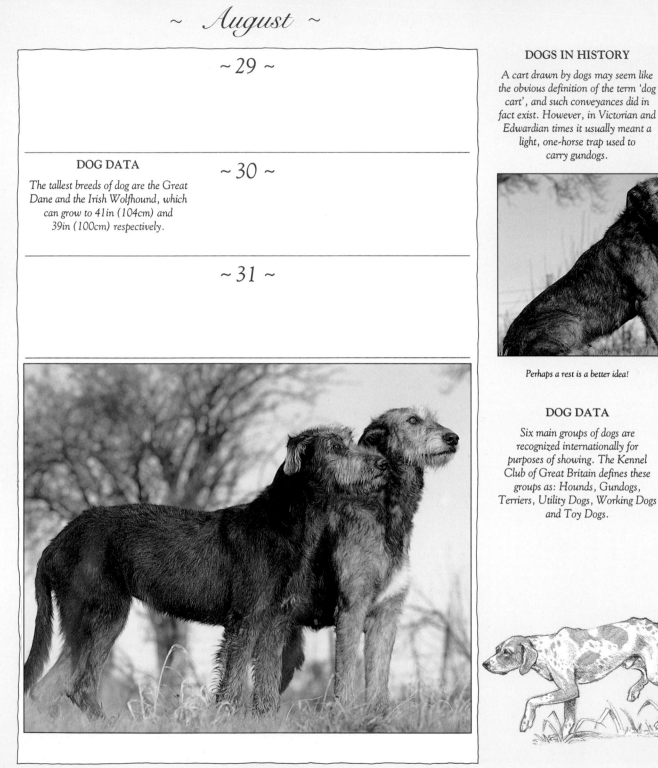

Ready for action: a handsome pair of Irish Wolfhounds.

'Gentle when stroked and fierce when provoked' sums up the ancient Irish Wolfhound.

~ *September* ~

I am his Highness' dog at Kew;
Pray tell me, sir, whose dog are you?

Inscription on the collar of a dog given to Frederick, Prince of
Wales, by Alexander Pope

Dalmatians at the ready.

~ September ~

DOGS' EPITAPHS

The Cemetery for Soldiers' Dogs in Edinburgh Castle, which received dogs for interment from 1742 until as recently as 1982, holds the remains of an unknown number of dogs who followed their masters into battle. Tombstones honour the memory of these brave and faithful companions, who surely showed devotion beyond the call of duty.

~ 1 ~

~ 2 ~

~ 3 ~

~ 4 ~

~ 5 ~

~ 6 ~

~ 7 ~

TOP DOGS

Greyhounds are the fastest dogs over distances of up to half a mile (0.8km), reaching a speed of 43mph (70kph). Beyond that distance the Whippet is faster, fractionally faster even than a very swift racehorse over a distance of 1.5 miles (2.4km). Another measure of the Whippet's speed is that it can take as little as 12 seconds to cover a distance of 200 yards (183m), while a trained athlete might take ten seconds to cover half that distance.

A maximum speed equalling that of the Greyhound – 43mph (70kph) – has been claimed for the Saluki, also known as the Gazelle Hound, but since the speeds of other breeds are seldom monitored as rigorously as those achieved by Greyhounds, the figure is difficult to verify.

The Greyhound, built for speed.

While wary of strangers, like many a breed the Greyhound is appreciative of its owner – and its companions.

~ 8 ~

~ 9 ~

~ 10 ~

~ 11 ~

~ 12 ~

~ 13 ~

~ 14 ~

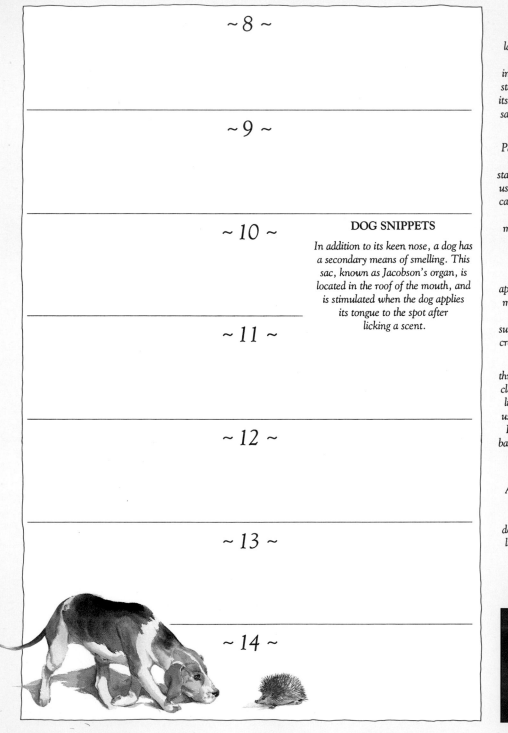

DOG SNIPPETS

In addition to its keen nose, a dog has a secondary means of smelling. This sac, known as Jacobson's organ, is located in the roof of the mouth, and is stimulated when the dog applies its tongue to the spot after licking a scent.

DOG DATA

Dogs employ an eloquent body language to express dominance and submission. The dominant dog intimidates its opponent with a fixed stare, bares its teeth in a snarl, holds its head high and moves stiffly. At the same time the hairs along the ridge of its back stand on end.

Paradoxically, by aggressive displays of this kind, in which it asserts its status as 'top dog', a dominant animal usually prevents a fight, since in most cases the other dog will back down. It is only when the unmistakable message of dominance is rejected by the opponent that a fight is likely to occur.

While the aggressive dog aims to appear larger by holding its head high, moving ponderously and making the fur on its back stand up, the submissive dog tries to look smaller by crouching and keeping its head down.

A ploy commonly used by a dog threatened with attack despite giving a clear message of submission, is to act like a puppy, since mature dogs are usually disinclined to attack puppies. In this display the dog rolls onto its back, exposing its genitals, and, in the ultimate gesture of submission, may even urinate

A similar message is conveyed by a quite different means when the submissive dog crawls up to the dominant animal and stretches up to lick its face. Once again, the dog is saying that it is a playful but harmless puppy.

A distinctively marked Bull Terrier.

A mix of breeds, including Bulldog and Dalmatian, the Bull Terrier is intelligent, obedient and pugnacious.

~ September ~

~ 15 ~

~ 16 ~

DOG DATA

The longest-lived dog on record was Bluey, a Queensland 'Heeler', an Australian cattle dog, who died in 1939 at the age of 29 years and five months.

~ 17 ~

~ 18 ~

~ 19 ~

~ 20 ~

~ 21 ~

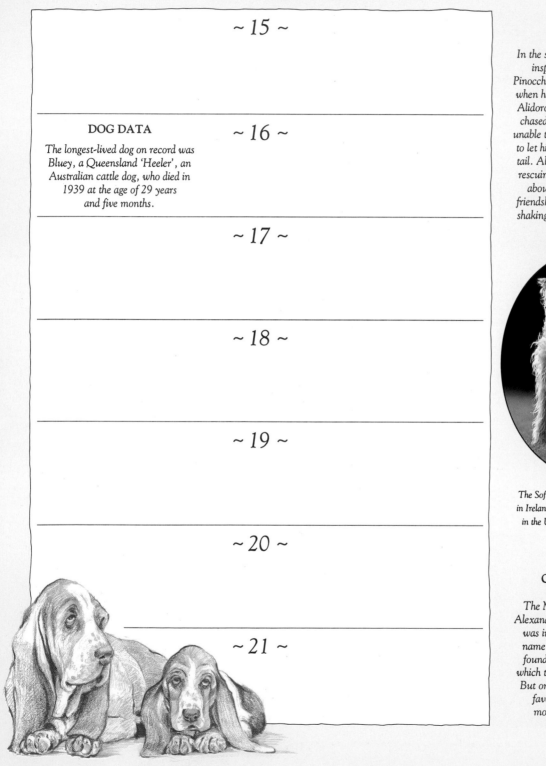

DOG TALES

Alidoro

In the story by Carlo Collodi which inspired Walt Disney's film, Pinocchio made an unexpected friend when he saved the life of the Mastiff Alidoro. Sent by the police, the dog chased Pinocchio into the sea, but unable to swim, he had no choice but to let himself be pulled ashore by his tail. Alidoro later repaid his debt by rescuing the wooden boy as he was about to be fried in flour, their friendship being sealed by Pinocchio shaking the dog's outstretched paw.

The Soft-coated Wheaten Terrier evolved in Ireland, but has found wider acceptance in the USA than in its country of origin or Britain.

CELEBRITY DOGS

The Macedonian empire-builder Alexander the Great (356-323 BC) was in the habit of bestowing the name Alexandria on the cities he founded on his trail of conquest, which took him as far east as India. But one he named Peritas, after a favourite dog, and erected a monument to the animal in the heart of the city.

An energetic and hardy breed, the Soft-coated Wheaten Terrier was first a farm dog, prized for its ratting skills.

DOG STARS

Bullet

Roy Rogers' canine companion in the 1951 film Spoilers of the Plain and the television series The Roy Rogers Show, which ran from that same year until 1964, was Bullet, a gifted Alsatian (German Shepherd). Although Bullet's repertoire included chases and various stunts, fight scenes were shot with a specially trained substitute.

After his death at Roy Rogers' ranch, Bullet was stuffed and is now on show alongside the cowboy's horse, Trigger, at the Roy Rogers-Dale Evans Museum in California.

~ 22 ~

~ 23 ~

~ 24 ~

~ 25 ~

~ 26 ~

~ 27 ~

~ 28 ~

DOG DATA

Nine of the best

Inevitably, the findings of Dr Oleson concerning dogs that bite (see March) were complemented by the research of fellow American Ernest L Abel, who discovered that the breeds least likely to bite are:

1 Golden Retriever
2 Labrador Retriever
3 Shetland Sheepdog
4 Old English Sheepdog
5 Welsh Terrier
6 Yorkshire Terrier
7 Beagle
8 Dalmatian
9 Pointer

Haute coiffure Yorkie style.

In the expressions of these Yorkshire Terrier puppies there is already a hint of the breed's plucky character.

~ *September* ~

~ 29 ~

~ 30 ~

Autumn days come quickly, like the running of the hound on the moor
Irish saying

One of Beatrix Potter's less well known tales, Ginger and Pickles , published in 1909, tells the salutary story of Pickles, a terrier, and Ginger, a tomcat, who together ran a village shop. Unfortunately, the pair's willingness to extend credit was matched by their customers' disinclination to ever settle their accounts. The result was that Pickles found himself with no money to pay for his dog licence. Cutting their losses, the pair ate the remains of their stock and closed the shop, and Pickles embarked on a new career as a gamekeeper.

A Dalmatian appealing to his owner.

This resting Dalmatian reveals the assured carriage of the head and the bright eye characteristic of the breed.

~ *October* ~

If you pick up a starving dog and make him prosperous, he will not bite you; that is the principal difference between a man and a dog.

Mark Twain (Samuel Langhorne Clemens) (1835-1910)

Keen not to miss out on anything, a Westie' bitch and her puppy keep their eyes straight ahead.

~ October ~

DOG DATA

In the 1990s the life expectancy of a dog in the developed countries is 11 or 12 years. Improved veterinary care and better feeding practices have steadily increased this figure, which at the turn of the century was seven years.

~ 1 ~

~ 2 ~

~ 3 ~

~ 4 ~

~ 5 ~

~ 6 ~

~ 7 ~

DOGS IN LEGEND AND MYTH

The guardian of Hades, the infernal region of classical mythology, was Cerberus, a monstrous dog with three heads: one of a dog, one of a wolf and one of a lion. His body was that of a Mastiff, his mane was a writhing mass of snakes and his tail was that of a dragon. Perhaps even worse, the watchdog had a treacherous dual nature, fawning on those who entered Hades but devouring those who tried to escape.

The story of Cerberus is, in fact, the subject of several myths. Hercules, after dragging the beast from the infernal regions to the earth, then let him go. Orpheus played his lyre to the fearsome dog, to lull him to sleep. Aeneas was conducted through Hades by the sibyl, who also sent the dog into a deep sleep, with a cake baked with poppies and honey.

It is probable that the myth of Cerberus has its origins even earlier, in ancient Egypt, where dogs were used to guard graves.

A Belgian Sheepdog takes a breather.

There are four breeds of Belgian Sheepdog: one of the loveliest, the Tervueren, is seen here.

~ *October* ~

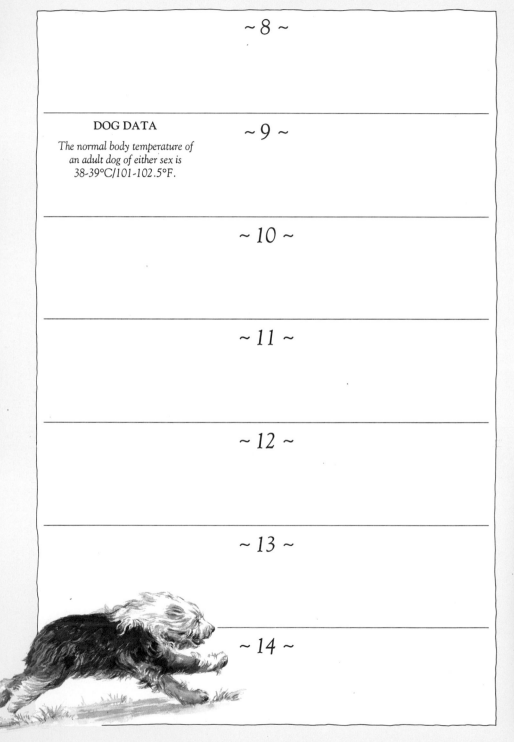

~ 8 ~

DOG DATA

*The normal body temperature of
an adult dog of either sex is
38-39°C/101-102.5°F.*

~ 9 ~

~ 10 ~

~ 11 ~

~ 12 ~

~ 13 ~

~ 14 ~

DOGS' EPITAPHS

Boatswain

*Lord Byron (1788-1824) honoured
the memory of his beloved
Newfoundland, Boatswain – who
was born in that province of Canada
in 1803 – by erecting a monument to
him at his family home, Newstead
Abbey, in Nottinghamshire, where
the dog died in front of the poet
in 1808.*

*Byron's inscription contains one of
the most moving tributes ever
addressed to a departed dog:*

*"Near this spot are deposited the
Remains of one Who possessed
Beauty without Vanity, Strength
without Insolence, Courage without
Ferocity, and all the Virtues of Man
without his Vices. This Praise, which
would be unmeaning flattery if
inscribed over Human Ashes, is but a
just tribute to the Memory of
Boatswain...'*

*A poem followed, ending with the
equally touching words:*

*Ye! who perchance behold this simple
urn, Pass on – it honours none you
wish to mourn: To mark a friend's
remains these stones arise; I never
knew but one – and here he lies.*

A Bearded Collie surveys the scene.

Bearded Collies are a lively breed, but with puppies to think about, this bitch needs to conserve her energy.

~ *October* ~

~ 15 ~

~ 16 ~

~ 17 ~

~ 18 ~

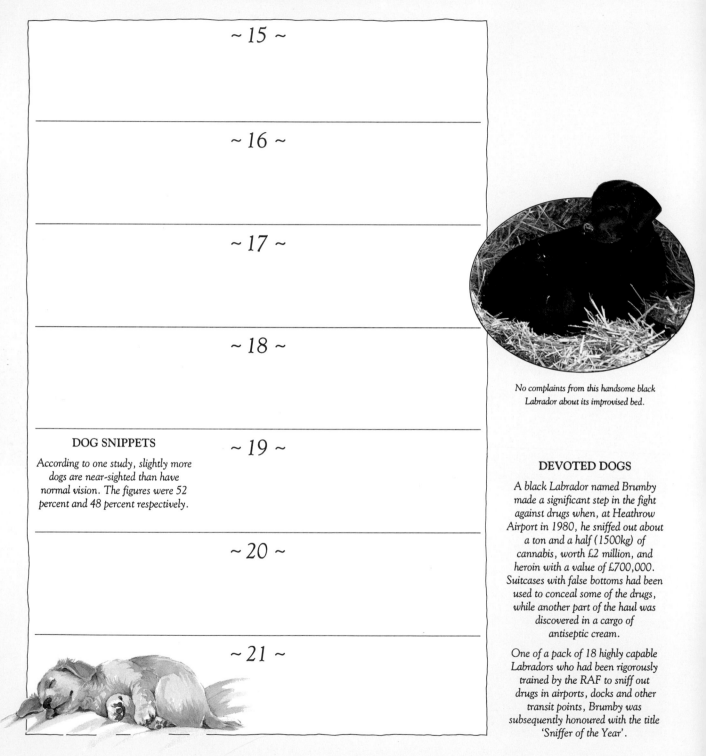

No complaints from this handsome black
Labrador about its improvised bed.

DOG SNIPPETS

~ 19 ~

*According to one study, slightly more
dogs are near-sighted than have
normal vision. The figures were 52
percent and 48 percent respectively.*

DEVOTED DOGS

*A black Labrador named Brumby
made a significant step in the fight
against drugs when, at Heathrow
Airport in 1980, he sniffed out about
a ton and a half (1500kg) of
cannabis, worth £2 million, and
heroin with a value of £700,000.
Suitcases with false bottoms had been
used to conceal some of the drugs,
while another part of the haul was
discovered in a cargo of
antiseptic cream.*

~ 20 ~

~ 21 ~

*One of a pack of 18 highly capable
Labradors who had been rigorously
trained by the RAF to sniff out
drugs in airports, docks and other
transit points, Brumby was
subsequently honoured with the title
'Sniffer of the Year'.*

Steady, dependable and loving, and a hard worker when trained, the Labrador is among the finest of companions.

DOG TALES

The Hound of the Baskervilles

In Sir Arthur Conan Doyle's gripping novel, published in 1902 and later made into a film, the spectral black hound of the title still stalks Dartmoor centuries after killing the evil Sir Hugo Baskerville and inflicting a curse on his descendants. Among these is Sir Charles Baskerville, who apparently dies of fright on encountering the beast. Sherlock Holmes investigates the mystery, and after hearing the fearsome creature savaging another victim on the bleak moor, the next night saves the life of Sir Henry Baskerville as he is about to suffer the same fate. Thus is finally laid the ghost of the fire-breathing beast.

~ 22 ~

~ 23 ~

~ 24 ~

~ 25 ~

~ 26 ~

~ 27 ~

~ 28 ~

TOP DOGS

While some American dog owners chase points at major dog shows in the USA, their British counterparts eagerly seek Challenge Certificates, or CCs as they are more often referred to in canine championship circles. To gain one CC is regarded by many dog lovers as an ample reward for their efforts.

However, Ch (Champion) U'Kwong King Solomon, also known as Solly, scooped an astounding 78 – the highest number of Challenge Certificates achieved by a British dog. The Chow Chow, who died in 1978 at ten years of age, was bred by Mrs Joan Egerton of Bramhall, Cheshire.

Won't someone play with me? this keen little 'Westie' seems to be asking.

An inquisitive outlook and great courage make the West Highland White Terrier an invaluable guard dog.

DOGS IN HISTORY

With its origins in the mid-17th century, the American Foxhound is the USA's oldest purebred dog. After settling in Maryland with his pack of Foxhounds, an Englishman, Robert Brooke, crossed his dogs with other Foxhounds from England, France and Ireland, to produce the American Foxhound.

~ 29 ~

~ 30 ~

~ 31 ~

Bright, responsive eyes and an apparently willing disposition can disguise the fact that the Foxhound requires throrough training and firm handling if it is to become fully obedient.

The American Foxhound is lighter in build and has a narrower chest than the English.

DOG TALES

John Joiner

Among Beatrix Potter's wonderful creations was the woodworking terrier, John Joiner. In The Roly-Poly Pudding, published in 1908, the brave little carpenter saves Tom Kitten from two rats who have trapped him under the floor of an attic. To show her gratitude to John Joiner for frightening off the kitten's tormentors with his furious sawing, Tabitha Twitchit invites him to dinner. Not surprisingly — for how often does a dog, even a fictional one, dine comfortably with a cat? — he declines, explaining that he has some hen coops to finish.

Like its American cousin, the English Foxhound is a dog of great strength and stamina – a true working breed.

~ *November* ~

Who finds me out both far and near
Tracing my footsteps every where
And when I whistle's sure to hear
My Rover

John Clare (1793-1864)

A Border Collie awaits instructions from his sheep-farming master.

~ November ~

~ 1 ~

~ 2 ~

DOG SNIPPETS

Japanese law requires that every champion Akita be declared a National Art Treasure and come under the government's protection.

~ 3 ~

~ 4 ~

~ 5 ~

~ 6 ~

~ 7 ~

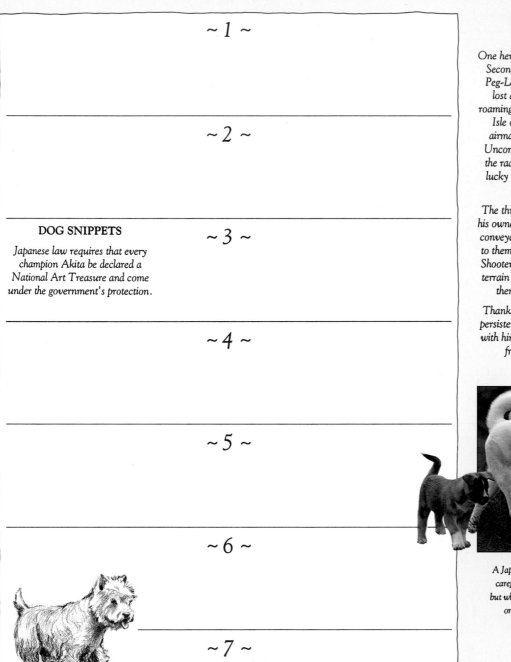

DEVOTED DOGS

Peg-Leg

One hero of the home front during the Second World War in Britain was Peg-Leg, so named because he had lost a leg as a puppy. One day, roaming the hills near his home on the Isle of Man, he came across an airman whose plane had ditched. Unconscious and seriously injured, the radio operator was nevertheless lucky to be alive, for the crash had killed his colleagues.

The three-legged dog hurried back to his owners, Mr and Mrs Shooter, and conveyed the urgency of the situation to them by his insistent barking. Mrs Shooter followed Peg-Leg over rough terrain to where the airman lay, and then summoned help for him.

Thanks to Peg-Leg's dedication and persistence, and his owners' empathy with him, the airman had been saved from certain death on the exposed hillside.

A Japanese Akita and her puppy tread carefully. Their colouring may differ but whatever colour it ends up, the little one will develop the double coat characteristic of the breed.

The Akita originated in the Polar region and was bred for hunting deer and wild boar.

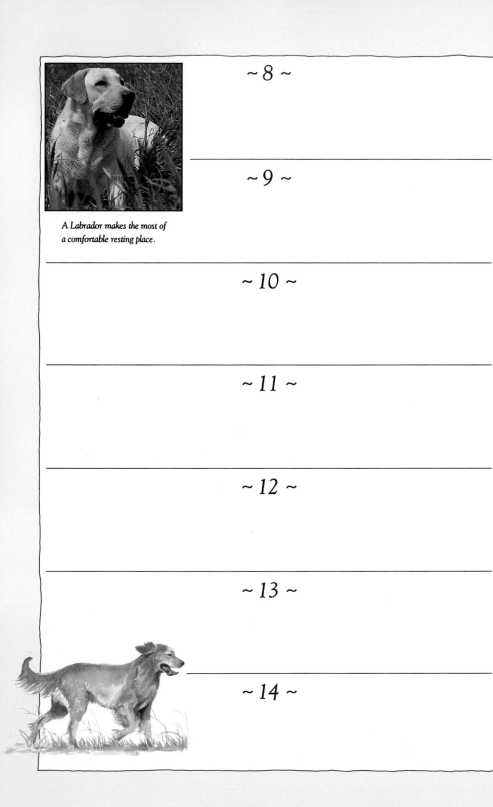

~ 8 ~

~ 9 ~

*A Labrador makes the most of
a comfortable resting place.*

~ 10 ~

~ 11 ~

~ 12 ~

~ 13 ~

~ 14 ~

DOGS IN HISTORY

The use of guide dogs by the blind can be traced back to the First World War, when a German doctor was struck by the caring attitude of an Alsatian (German Shepherd) towards a blind patient. To investigate the use of dogs in this way, the doctor set up an experimental centre.

Mrs Dorothy Harrison Eustis, a wealthy American who was at that time training Alsatians in Switzerland for army and police use, wrote about the German dog-training centre in an article which attracted the attention of a blind American, Morris Frank. Later Mr Frank was to own Buddy, the first dog to be trained successfully by Mrs Eustis, and the first guide dog in the USA.

In 1928 Mrs Eustis set up L'Oeil Qui Voit (The Seeing Eye) in Vevey, Switzerland, and, the following year in Nashville, Tennessee, the first guide-dog school in America: The Seeing Eye, Inc.

As a result of meeting Mrs Eustis in England, Mrs Muriel Crooke and Mrs Rosamund Bond, who were both involved in breeding and training dogs, started the first training classes for guide dogs in the country, in Wallasey, near Liverpool. It was these pioneering classes that led, in 1934, to the creation of Britain's Guide Dogs for the Blind Association.

Nowadays the breeds trained for use by the blind include the Alsatian, but more commonly used are Labrador/ Retriever crosses, Labrador Retrievers and Golden Retrievers. Less often, dogs of the collie type are used. A dog usually starts its training at one year, and is assigned to its new owner three or four months later. Eight or nine years is the average working life of a guide dog, many living on to enjoy their retirement.

Not 'golden' – the description is restricted to Retrievers – this Labrador is correctly referred to as 'yellow'.

~ 15 ~

~ 16 ~

~ 17 ~

~ 18 ~

~ 19 ~

~ 20 ~

~ 21 ~

The Scottish Terrier is a cheerful and adaptable little dog, but in most cases not without a strong streak of independence which reveals itself every once in a while.

DOGS IN ART

In medieval art dogs frequently symbolize fidelity. Dogs are seen lying at the feet of Saints Bernard, Benignus and Wendelon, carrying a lighted torch in depictions of St Dominic and licking the wounds of St Roch.

Statues of many of the Crusaders represent them with their foot on a dog, to show that they followed the precepts of the Lord as faithfully as a dog follows the footsteps of his master

A dog lying at the feet of a woman was used in monuments to symbolize both affection and fidelity – a tradition which continued until at least the Victorian era.

DOG DATA

Since the earliest times, breeds of dog with especially acute noses have been used to track prey, and nowadays keen-nosed dogs, mostly Alsatians (German Shepherds), are used to sniff out felons, drugs and gas leaks.

But their role in other areas, such as detecting mines and explosives, is fast being usurped by the pig. This fact may well produce a Gallic shrug from the French, who at one time used pigs to search out truffles from among tree roots.

In the opinion of the English author Rudyard Kipling (1865-1936) the pig was 'an appetite at the end of a rope' while the truffle hound was 'an artiste to all appearances which is studious in dedicating itself to its art'. It is certainly true that dogs now find greater favour among truffle hunters for the compelling reason that they are easier to train not to eat the 'black gold'.

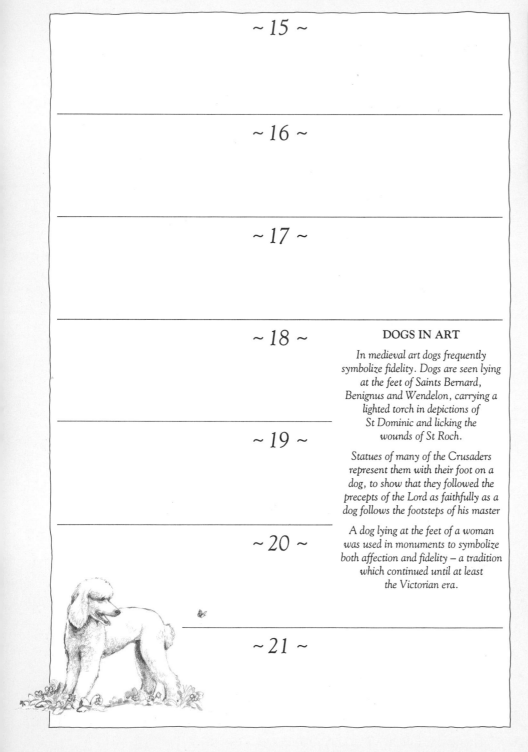

The old saying, 'Once a Scottie owner, always a Scottie owner' is heartily endorsed by owners of these terrier

~ *November* ~

~ 22 ~

~ 23 ~

~ 24 ~

~ 25 ~

~ 26 ~

DOGS IN LEGEND AND MYTH

A Chinese myth tells of a dog called Tien-Kow who howls in the heavens and, by eating the sun or the moon, causes an eclipse.

~ 27 ~

~ 28 ~

DOGS IN ART

When Sir Edwin Landseer saw Paul Pry for the first time, in 1838, the black and white Newfoundland was carrying a basket of flowers in his mouth. So struck by Paul Pry's beauty was the great Victorian animal painter that he bequeathed the dog to posterity by painting a fine studio portrait of him, A Distinguished Member of the Humane Society.

The artist dedicated the picture, which shows Paul Pry on a stone wall with the sea behind him, to Britain's Royal Humane Society. An engraving based on it was so popular that ever since that time black and white Newfoundlands have been known as Landseers.

For centuries the Pekingese was a firm favourite at the Imperial Palace in what is now Beijing. But since the last century the breed has become almost extinct in China.

Loyal, courageous and fierce in defence of its owner, the tiny Pekingese is valued for its big personality.

~ 29 ~

DOG LORE

Dog grass, another name for couch grass, is so called because dogs which have lost their appetite eat it as an emetic and purgative.

DOG SAYINGS

~ 30 ~

It's a bad hound that's not worth the whistling
Irish proverb

The Airedale Terrier's origins can be traced back to the valley of the River Aire in Yorkshire, where it was bred from the Otterhound, the Old English Terrier and the Welsh Terrier.

The Airedale Terrier displays an attractive blend of black and tan.

Hardy, affectionate and intelligent, the Airedale is for many the 'King of Terriers'.

~ *December* ~

If it be the chief point of friendship to comply with a friend's motions and inclinations, he possesses this in an eminent degree; he lies down when I sit, and walks when I walk, which is more than many good friends can pretend to.

Alexander Pope (1688-1744), in a letter describing his dog

The Shar-Pei ranks among the rarest dogs in the world.

~ *December* ~

~ 1 ~

~ 2 ~

DOG SNIPPETS

The dog-loving English poet and essayist Alexander Pope (1688-1744) gave the following sanguine advice in his An Essay on Man: 'Go, like the Indian, in another life Expect thy dog, thy bottle, and thy wife.'

~ 3 ~

~ 4 ~

~ 5 ~

~ 6 ~

~ 7 ~

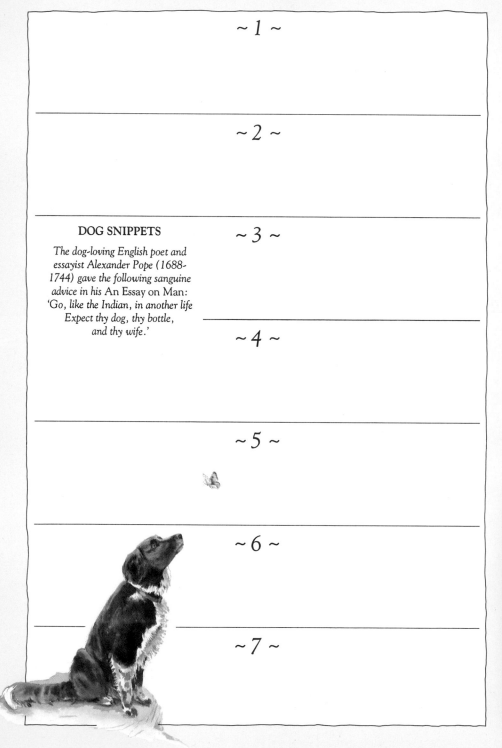

DOG TALES

Lassie

In 1938 Eric Knight published a short story in the Saturday Evening Post about a Collie who makes an epic journey of hundreds of miles, suffering misfortune and harsh treatment along the way, to find her original owner, young Joe, whose father had sold her when he lost his job.

So popular was the story that two years later the author published it as a book, which before long had appeared in 25 languages. The touching story of devotion exceptional even for a dog, inspired the 1943 film Lassie Come Home and its sequels, as well as much-loved radio and television series.

Pal, a male, played the title role in Lassie Come Home, when the female who was to play the part began to moult during the filming, which was taking place in summer. This was the start of a successful career for Pal, who appeared in seven of the eight Lassie films, the last of which was The Magic of Lassie (1978).

A good-looking Rough Collie.

From its origins as a Scottish herding dog, the Rough Collie has become a worldwide favourite.

~ December ~

~ 8 ~

A playful Cairn Terrier.

~ 9 ~

~ 10 ~

~ 11 ~

~ 12 ~

CELEBRITY DOGS

Cherami

Louis XI (1423-83) doted on his favourite Greyhound, Cherami, to the extent of having a gold collar studded with rubies made for him.

~ 13 ~

~ 14 ~

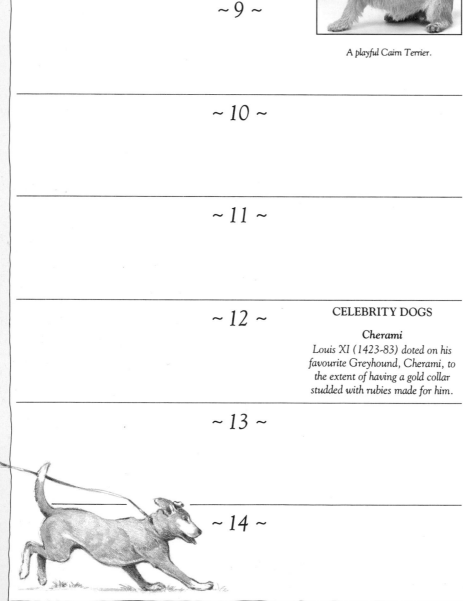

DOGS IN ART

There are many paintings, by artists of all periods, in which a dog (or dogs) is an adjunct to the main subject. Less common, but by no means unusual, is the portrait of a dog alone.

Without doubt the best known, and certainly one of the most prolific painters of dogs was the Victorian artist Sir Edwin Landseer (1802-73), who produced dozens, if not hundreds, of canvases featuring dogs.

Among the many dogs of his own who sat for Landseer were: a white Terrier mongrel, Brutus; Brechin, a rather dim-witted dog who drowned at sea; Lassie and Myrtle, a Scottish Sheepdog and a Retriever; Lion, a St Bernard measuring 6ft 4in (1.93m) in length and 2ft 7in (79cm) in height at the dip in his back; and Caesar, another St Bernard.

Among the other famous painters who have portrayed dogs, either with their owner or as the main subject, are: Hieronymous Bosch (c. 1450-1516) in Pedlar, *Pieter Brueghel (c.1525-69) in* Hunters in the Snow *, Goya (1746-1828) in* Parasol *, Hogarth (1697-1764) in* William Hogarth with his Dog *,* Reynolds *(1723-92) in* Miss Bowler and her Spaniel, *Renoir (1841-1919) in* Madame Charpentier and her Children *, Rubens (1577-1640) in* The Chateau de Steen, *Titian (c. 1487/90-1576) in* Bacchus and Ariadne, *Veronese (c. 1528-88) in* An Allegory of Love *and Watteau (1684-1721) in* Enseigne de Gersaint.

A fearless little dog, the Norwich Terrier is blessed with a happy disposition too – all in all a great companion.

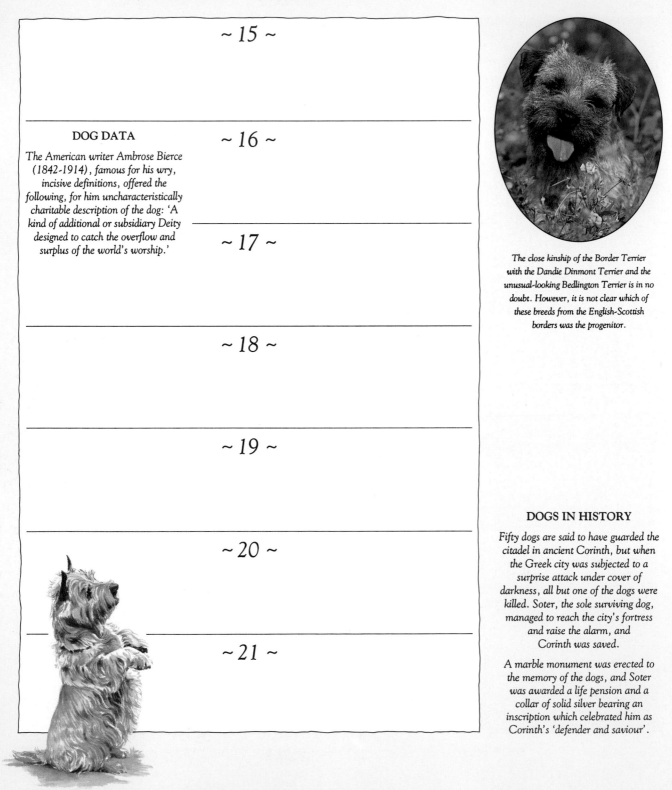

~ 15 ~

~ 16 ~

~ 17 ~

~ 18 ~

~ 19 ~

~ 20 ~

~ 21 ~

DOG DATA

The American writer Ambrose Bierce (1842-1914), famous for his wry, incisive definitions, offered the following, for him uncharacteristically charitable description of the dog: 'A kind of additional or subsidiary Deity designed to catch the overflow and surplus of the world's worship.'

The close kinship of the Border Terrier with the Dandie Dinmont Terrier and the unusual-looking Bedlington Terrier is in no doubt. However, it is not clear which of these breeds from the English-Scottish borders was the progenitor.

DOGS IN HISTORY

Fifty dogs are said to have guarded the citadel in ancient Corinth, but when the Greek city was subjected to a surprise attack under cover of darkness, all but one of the dogs were killed. Soter, the sole surviving dog, managed to reach the city's fortress and raise the alarm, and Corinth was saved.

A marble monument was erected to the memory of the dogs, and Soter was awarded a life pension and a collar of solid silver bearing an inscription which celebrated him as Corinth's 'defender and saviour'.

The adaptable Border Terrier is as happy playing with children as he is on a hard day's hunting in the hills.

~ 22 ~

~ 23 ~

~ 24 ~

~ 25 ~

~ 26 ~

~ 27 ~

~ 28 ~

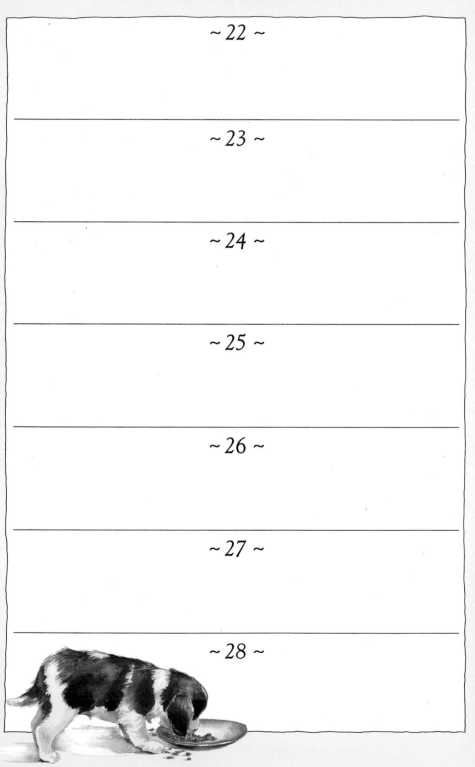

DOG BREEDS

The Polar Group

The dogs best equipped to contend with extreme cold belong to the Polar or Spitz group, which includes Alaskan and Siberian Huskies, Canadian and Greenland Eskimo Dogs, the Norwegian Elkhound and the Alaskan Malamute. Of these, the last is the toughest, as well as the biggest, and can haul hundreds of pounds for hours on end in temperatures as much as 94°F (35°C) below zero.

An ancestor of the Polar group was the Peat Dog, which appeared in the nomadic communities of the Arctic Circle in the Neolithic era, 7000-8000 years ago. The breed spread right across Europe, later gaining the alternative name of the Swiss Lake Dweller Dog. Related to the wolf, it probably most closely resembled the Samoyed.

The wolf-like Siberian Husky.

A young Siberian Husky directs his piercing blue eyes at the intruder into his habitat.

~ *December* ~

DOG DATA

No one would dispute the fact that dogs have a much stronger sense of smell than humans, although scientists disagree on how much keener the canine nose is. The most common estimate grants dogs a sense of smell 40 times as powerful as a human's, and others put it at 100 times, while an eminent French animal behaviourist claims that a million times is a more accurate figure.

~ 29 ~

~ 30 ~

~ 31 ~

Despite its size, the Bernese Mountain dog seldom shows hostility to other dogs.

DOGS IN HISTORY

The notion of the St Bernard carrying a tiny barrel of brandy around its neck is not based on fact. It was an invention of the British painter of sentimental pictures of animals, Sir Edwin Landseer, who incorporated the detail in his painting of 1820 Alpine Mastiffs Reanimating a Traveller.

In Switzerland the Bernese Mountain Dog has been used for herding, droving, guarding and as a draught dog.

~ *Aquarius* ~

January 21st – February 19th
The sign of the WATER BEARER

Tolerant, reserved, idealistic

*The Aquarian pooch is in a league of his own –
and if your pet was born under this sign this will
probably come as a great relief. No other
companion is as lively – mentally, that is –
don't expect good odds at the track with this dog
for it is in his bed, or 'laboratory', as he likes to
call it, that he exerts himself. A real maelstrom
of subversive activity seethes between those
widely spaced eyes and strange, pointy ears.*

*Original thinkers and natural inventors, it will
doubtless be a dog ruled by Uranus that is the
first to open a tin of chunks. He will accomplish
this chiefly because of his hunger for success,
however, as the Aquarian dog often has a
moody relationship with food, brought about by
his inability to lower himself from science to
nature. This inability can also hinder the
intimacy of his relationships. It's not that he
doesn't like people, he does – all of them, to the
same degree. His lack of passionate
commitment and an aversion to having his ears
rubbed make him an unattractive proposition to
the sentimental dog lover, but his gregarious
nature makes him a friendly, loyal and
trustworthy family pet.*

Compatible signs: *Libra and Gemini*

~ *Pisces* ~

February 20th – March 20th
The sign of the FISH

Imaginative, peace-loving and kind

*The dog born in Pisces is a dreamer, a
philosopher, a spiritualist. That's why his big,
limpid eyes seem to have unfathomable depths:
inside his head is all the Universe, yet Chaos
too. A somewhat ethereal creature, therefore,
the dog ruled by Neptune is a delightfully fey pet
that will prove a loving companion.*

*His submissive nature and self-sacrificing
devotion make him susceptible to having his toes
trodden on, however, and sensitivity is needed
to keep this fishy fellow happy. Unlike the
Aquarian, this dog needs lots of input, direction
– identity, even – or he will drift and possibly
become morose, for there is a duality in this sign
which can produce a perverse inversion of these
usually kind-natured dogs. Nor does the Piscean
pooch withstand criticism; he is greatly upset by
a bad atmosphere and a careless word may send
him retreating, wounded, into the fantasy world
of his imagination where all is peaceful and a
bowl of warm milk ever present. Small of frame
and delicate-looking, the Piscean dog is
deceptively hardy and will usually live a long
life. As would be expected, he is an
excellent swimmer.*

Compatible signs: *Cancer and Scorpio*

~ Aries ~

March 21st – April 20th
The sign of the RAM

New beginnings, energy, leadership

Aries is the sign of energy, courage and reckless boisterousness. This is not a dog for a one-bedroomed flat. Nor, despite his undeniable qualities of leadership, would his impulsive, self-seeking, 'Devil take the high road' attitude recommend him as a guide dog for the blind. Like the Ram, the symbol of Aries, the dog born under Mars will stop at nothing short of concussion to see that his will be done. Along with Sagittarius, this sign governs the destruction of kitchen doors and the chewing of tethers. The Arien dog must be allowed to follow his feckless passions and get out there into the park where the action is, whether it be in the shape of a leggy lady Labrador or a confrontation with a mongrel who doesn't give him precedence at the lampost.

The Arien dog's fiery energy may show as aggression on occasion but it is irrepressible and will not diminish with age. Veterinary insurance is advisable, along with early castration, since these dogs are known to love a fight over a female. The Arien pet is best suited to the owner with spacious grounds and a stout heart, to whom he'll be a source of great pleasure.

Compatible signs: *Leo and Sagittarius*

~ Taurus ~

(April 21st – May 21st)
The sign of the BULL

Steadfast, courageous and firm

The personality of the dog born a Taurean makes it an ideal house pet, for none other could be as home-loving, reliable and loyal. He is also sturdily courageous, jealously defensive and methodical. As a guard dog he will make tours of the perimeter every hour on the hour and woe betide an intruder for, as the Bull of the Zodiac, this sign may change from his customary placidity to powerful rage in a flash. Born under the sign most closely bound to nature, the Taurean dog will very likely be happier in the country than in the town, where the pace is that little bit too fast for his conservative tastes (which are simple and involve a high calorie intake).

The Taurean dog's highly developed sensuality – he will dribble with delight as you tickle his overly round tummy – may become slothfulness and gluttony in later life; difficulty could easily be encountered shifting him from the hearth. His lack of imagination doesn't help, but you will forgive him this as you look in his trusting, dependable, square face. After all, he's one of the Zodiac's true 'best friends'.

Compatible signs: *Virgo and Capricorn*

~ Gemini ~

May 22nd – June 21st
The sign of the TWINS

Duality, versatility, the intellect

Most dogs called 'Sparky' are born in Gemini, for that sums up their nature; quick, dextrous, and bright. This Geminian dog is intelligent and likes everyone to know it. Consequently he is very good at tricks, though he is nobody's fool and operates strictly on his own terms, which sometimes leaves people wondering just who is the master in the house where he resides.

The dog born in Gemini is ruled by Mercury and possesses the quicksilver properties of that metal, but not its characteristic melting response to warmth. These dogs are not much given to cuddles and display an almost clinical detachment at times, being more 'mental' than sentimental. Nervous energy manifests itself as restlessness and agitation if the Geminian dog is under-excercised and breakables should be kept well out of the way, as should favourite slippers lest they be chewed in frustration. Often prone to excessive barking, these dogs love the sound of their own voices and this may become a little wearing. However, the Gemini dog's versatility and lively charm make him a very good pet for the owner who understands his sometimes perverse nature.

Compatible signs: *Aquarius and Libra*

~ Cancer ~

June 22nd – July 23rd
The sign of the CRAB

Sensitive, maternal and very romantic

A puppy born under this sign is a loyal, domesticated, stay-at-home dog who sees it as his responsibility to look after his household to the best of his considerable abilities. Nurturing and protective, these dogs are excellent with children and pups alike (as with Aries, an early visit to the vets is suggested as these dog are born to reproduce). Like the Crab, the symbol of Cancer, these dogs are very defensive and possess enormous tenacity, especially when their security is threatened. The Cancerian dog will guard 'his' (your) family with his life. Postmen fear these dogs for good reason for, like the claws of the crab, such animals do not readily release their grip. Early training should guide the Cancerian dog gently towards differentiating between friend and foe or misunderstandings may occur and legal fees build up.

A healthy appetite coupled with a reluctance to exercise usually results in these dogs becoming overweight, so, much as he will try to blackmail you out of it, be careful with his feeding and encourage his aptitude for swimming, should the opportunity arise.

Compatible signs: *Pisces and Scorpio*

~ *Leo* ~

July 24th – August 23rd
The sign of the LION

Self-confidence, enthusiasm, pride

Abundant warmth, generosity and fur characterise the Leonine dog, probably the most demanding hound in the Zodiac. He will go to great lengths to impress his owner (and everyone else), which makes him an ideal showdog. His vanity, arrogance and insatiable thirst for flattery also commend him to this path. In addition, dogs born under this sign often display a fiery gold tint in their coats which distinguishes them as the Kings of the Zodiacal jungle. Failing that, the condition of the coat – usually exceptionally glossy – will find the Leo canine head and shoulders above the rest.

If the Leo dog is one of several in the household care should be taken that his domineering nature does not oppress other more pensive pups. Discipline is something he simply does not comprehend – just why should he do as you say? Treated with respect and admiration, though, (which is inspired by these often large, fearless-looking dogs) he is a loving and rewarding companion, always noticed by his owner's friends. These dogs ruled by the Sun make excellent parents, taking a singular pride in their offspring; they are therefore good stud dogs, being both noble and gracious.

Compatible signs: *Aries and Sagittarius*

~ *Virgo* ~

August 24th – September 23rd
The sign of the VIRGIN

Discriminative, methodical, logical

The Virgoan dog is a keen worker, dependable and bright with a down-to-earth conformity that makes him an appealing proposition to someone who perhaps hasn't got the time for a more demanding pooch. Indeed, the Virgoan dog is not always that keen on attention; his independent streak may make him appear a little stand-offish at times. But he has charm and is eager to please his owner in more practical ways that as a mere lap dog.

His subdued sense of adventure would make him an excellent rescue dog if only he didn't dislike getting dirty so much, for he is very fussy about cleanliness. A constant groomer, the Virgoan dog is deeply distressed by mess of any sort – it disturbs the order of his mind. Perhaps, therefore, he would be better suited to police work, where he could combine his need to serve with a little detection and logic and gain the respect (he cares little for love) he longs for. A picky eater, this dog's diet needs monitoring or digestive disorders may occur. Tempt him with small, tasty meals, designed to appeal to his discrminating palate.

Compatible signs: *Taurus and Capricorn*

(September 24th – October 23rd)
The sign of the SCALES

Balance, justice, love of beauty

The Libran dog is highly sociable and easily spotted by the welcoming grin with which he charms all visitors alike, whether they be burglars or clergy – he is at least democratic, if not shrewd. Very friendly, the Libran dog's craving to be loved makes him most appealing, even though you know he is quite undiscerning and self-motivated. Yet he is sensitve to his owner's moods and will tune into and adjust himself to their feelings, which makes him an ideal companion for the housebound or lonely.

Very fond of luxury, this dog does demand a high standard of living and will instinctively seek out the most comfortable chair and not take kindly to being told to budge. The symbol of Libra, the Scales, represents peace, balance, harmony and beauty. The Libran canine is therefore a peaceful creature who exudes a quiet calm that should not be taken for laziness. A dog much given to esoteric ponderings (naps), the scales of his finely balanced mind may tip towards melancholia as well as elation, but this is soon rectified by a compliment, a kind word, or, if all else fails, a recital of Beethoven's Ninth Symphony.

October 24th – November 22nd
The sign of the SCORPION

Tenacious, secretive, intensly psychic

There is something dark in the psyche of the dog born under Scorpio which will always remain unfathomable to his owner. Scorpio is ruled by Pluto, the most distant of the planets, and it is perhaps for this reason that the dogs born at this time are a bit mysterious. They are certainly intense, emotional creatures prone to secrecy, suspicion and vengeance. Never slight your Scorpio dog, especially if his tail is long and pointy....

Often in possession of an inhibiting stare and a fine pair of shoulders, a couple of these dogs would deter most would-be intruders without moving a muscle. Not a playful mutt, the Scorpio dog has enormous self-control – that is until something, inevitably, gives. When this happens it is safer to be on the other side of a thick door. These dogs are usually very attractive to the opposite sex, often seeking and finding unsuitable partners regardless of their owner's wishes. At home their powerful energy is a strong force in the household. If kept happy a Scorpio dog will be a loyal companion – as long as you don't expect him to play with squeaky toys.

Compatible signs: *Aquarius and Gemini*   **Compatible signs:** *Cancer and Pisces*

~ *Sagittarius* ~

November 23rd – December 21st
The sign of the ARCHER

Extrovert, optimistic, independent

The puppy born in Sagittarius is never a dull dog; he is boisterous, independent and enthusiastic, following the symbol of this sign, a speeding arrow from a Centaur's bow. This is why he runs off a lot on walks, returning dishevelled and exhausted days later. He is not a dog for the faint-hearted or protective owner, therefore, who would never rest for worry of what adventure their precious pup was engaged in from one moment to the next. Happiest with lots of space to roam, these dogs are probably safer in the countryside, as six-lane carriageways will not deter them from their quarry (usually imaginary, sometimes feline).

Often of large, gangly frame, the Sagittarian canine is built to be outward bound, not treading carpet, and has no respect for china, which gets broken regularly by his exuberant tail-wagging. These dogs revel in attention and are great performers, playing for hours with their toys – in which the owner should invest wholesale if he attempts to keep the Sagittarian dog indoors for more than two hours at a time. A lovable and constant companion, this dog is well suited to the active family.

Compatible signs: *Aries and Leo*

~ *Capricorn* ~

December 22nd – January 20th
The sign of the GOAT

Industrious, meticulous, persevering

Even as a puppy the Capricorn does not possess the expected doggy optimism and vitality usual in the species. It is as if he's been here before in other lives, he's resigned to it, will not be surprised and finds the other dogs rather rude. He is strong of character and also ambitious and possesses a 'dog-ged' determination to achieve. His even temper, sensibility and industrious nature would suit him to the life of a working Sheepdog, where he would enjoy his superiority over the herd and respect his master's guidance.

His good sense makes him a little cautious, but nevertheless the Capricorn dog is undyingly faithful if his master is deserving. Greyfriar's Bobby was no doubt one such dog born under this sign. Though there is little of sentiment in the goaty personality, the Capricorn dog is reliable of temperament and ideal for the family with young children, who will learn how best to live with a pet from his dignified stoicism and wisdom, while being sheltered by his calm, unruffled affection for them.

Compatible signs: *Taurus and Virgo*